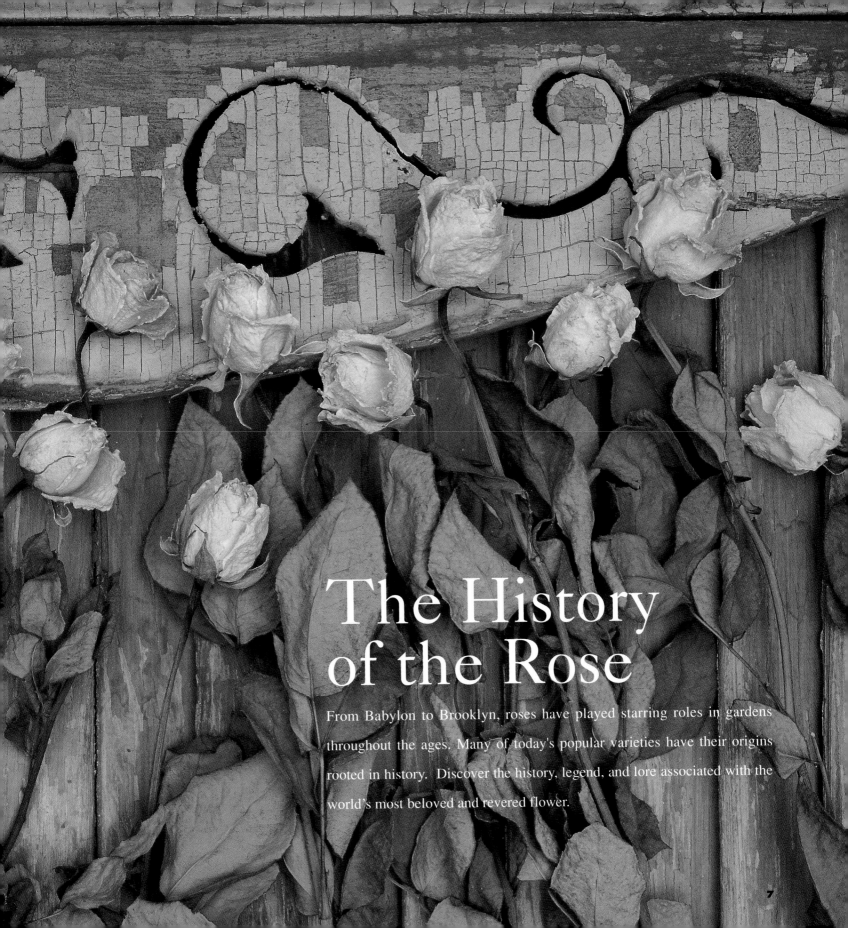

The History of the Rose

From Babylon to Brooklyn, roses have played starring roles in gardens throughout the ages. Many of today's popular varieties have their origins rooted in history. Discover the history, legend, and lore associated with the world's most beloved and revered flower.

The History of the Rose

Throughout the ages, the form and flower of the rose have symbolized intangible beauty and power. Its gentle blooms graced the paths of many ancient civilizations: Roman emperors, Egyptian queens, and kings in China all coveted the rose as a symbol of perfection and opulence. No other flower has been so replicated in art. For centuries, rose motifs have been used lavishly in paintings, tapestries, and ceramics. In literature, the rose has been elevated by poets and writers to be the dominant symbol of purity and romantic love. And it was the emblem of the rose that was borne into battle during the 15th-century Wars of the Roses, the clash between the Houses of York and Lancaster. King Henry VII superimposed the red rose of Lancaster with the white rose of York to create the Tudor rose, a red-and-white rose that came to symbolize unity.

Since first discovered, this simple flower has evoked complex responses: Its beauty inspired poetry to heal the spirit; its leaves and hips produced medicines to cure the body; and its petals produced oils to anoint the blessed. Proclaimed the "queen of flowers," the rose is a fitting symbol of civilization. From robust canes, the persistent rose blooms year after year, bearing supple, delicate, and often fragrant flowers. In the garden, the rose is both conquering hero and delicate maiden. Its form conjures all the passion that myth and literature have attributed to it. Revered throughout time for its sensual beauty, the rose remains a favorite among gardeners for its variety of color, its versatility of form, and its rich fragrance.

The Myth and Power of the Rose

The rose is a central theme in the myths, stories, and poetry of many cultures. In Greek and Roman mythology, the rose represented emotions from passion to modesty. Droplets of blood from Venus, the goddess of love and beauty, were thought to have spawned the first red roses. Pink roses, to match the modest blushes of a maiden, were the gift of Bacchus, the god of wine. In other stories, the rose was said to have been born from the smile of Cupid. The expression "sub rosa" (under the rose) refers to the ancient association the rose has with secrecy. In Middle Eastern mythology, Allah created the white rose because the lotus slept at night. Medieval legends hold that a white rose bloomed in the Garden of Eden, and was turned blush after a kiss from Eve.

Poets have long used the rose for its metaphorical flexibility. The power of the rose and its symbolic relation to beauty, innocence, youth, and goodness dominate poetry and literature. Shakespeare described the rose as "that sweet ornament which truth doth give!" The rose symbolizes the fleeting of time; we are reminded by Robert Herrick to "Gather ye rosebuds while ye may, Old Time is still a-flying." Emily Brontë's rose symbolized time's theft of youth and beauty: "The wild rose-briar is sweet in spring,

Its summer blossoms scent the air; Yet wait til winter comes again And who will call the wild-briar fair?"

But above all, in poetry the rose most often is compared to the fairness of a beloved, as in Robert Burns' lines, "my luve is like a red, red rose, That's newly sprung in June."

> Oh, no Man knows Through what wild centuries Roves back the rose!
>
> — Walter de la Mare

The rose as a symbol is so compatible to literary device, in part, because of its origins. The rose is a testament to man's creativity; once a wild flower, the rose has been cultivated and engineered to suit the needs of all types of gardens and landscapes. From formal rose gardens resplendent with the patrician blooms of hybrid teas to rocky walls covered with rambling roses galloping away in bloom, roses embody the passion, strength, and stamina so admired by poets and gardeners alike.

The image of the rose is widely depicted in art. The earliest representation of the flower appeared in frescoes at the Palace of Knossos in Crete, which date from 2000–1700 B.C. From that time on, the elegant form of the rose was forged into metal and coins, woven into tapestries, and hand-painted onto china. Glorious bouquets of roses were painted by Dutch painters such as Jan Brueghel the Elder in the 16th century. The rose remained a favorite subject for painters for several centuries.

The rose paintings of the 18th century influenced the simple and elegant rose watercolors of the botanical illustrator Pierre-Joseph Redouté. Redouté was commissioned by Empress Josephine, wife of Napoleon, to paint the roses in her garden at the Palace of Malmaison. Josephine's rose collection was the greatest and most extensive of its day, including more than 200 varieties. The roses of Malmaison were recorded in LES ROSES, published in 1817, which was the definitive standard for rose botanicals of its time.

The rose motif spoke the language of beauty and symmetry. Great European cathedrals built in the 12th century paid artistic homage to the beauty of the rose by incorporating the extraordinary rose window as an architectural scheme. Roses were carved over confessionals and into the ceilings of council chambers to symbolize secrecy. Roses and rosettes were used widely as ornaments in furniture. And in 16th-century England, the rose and crown emblem was stamped into the highest-quality pewter; the rose then came to represent superior quality along with all its other virtues.

The adoration of the rose reached its zenith in the 19th century. The Victorians elevated the use of roses both in decoration and in the garden. During this period, great numbers of new rose varieties were developed, and rose gardening blossomed into an obsession in Europe and America. The Victorian rose garden was an enchanted respite for private reflection and a stage for public display. With the advent of the printed valentine, roses gained a vernacular of their own. In the language of the rose, the red rose said "I love you," the yellow rose revealed declining love and jealousy, and the white rose's meaning translated into a demure statement of worthiness.

The custom of naming a rose after a distinguished person or celebrity shows the power of the rose by the company it keeps. For years, rose breeders have bestowed the name of their loved ones on their rose creations. The elegant white 'Madame Hardy' was introduced by J. A. Hardy to honor his wife. 'Souvenir de la Malmaison,' the delicate pink rose, pays tribute to Empress Josephine and the extraordinary rose collection in her garden at Malmaison. This tradition of honor has continued into modern times with roses being named after personalities such as John F. Kennedy, Barbara Bush, Cary Grant, Bing Crosby, Lucille Ball, Dorothy Perkins, Whoopi Goldberg, and rosarians Graham Thomas and Gertrude Jekyll.

Origins of the Rose

Fossilized rose leaves dating to prehistoric times prove that roses have existed longer than man. No one knows when in the life history of the rose that it was discovered, but from that time onward, no other flower has been paid so high a tribute.

Ancient cultures were responsible for the cultivation and the popularity of the rose. The gardens of the pharaohs bloomed with roses. The Romans

The red rose
whispers of passion,
And the white rose
breathes of love;
Oh, the red rose
is a falcon, And
the white rose
is a dove.

— John Boyle O'Reilly

cultivated roses for gardens and grew them as crops for their petals, which were used to make rose tarts and perfumed wine. Emperor Nero's appetite for roses was insatiable: The floors of his banquet halls were strewn with petals and his cushions were stuffed with them, while fountains bubbled over with rose water. Cleopatra entertained Mark Antony in a room filled knee-high with rose petals.

Rose gardens existed in China as early as 2700 B.C. The Hanging Gardens of Babylon, created by King Nebuchadnezzar around 500 B.C., likely contained roses. During medieval times roses were valued for their culinary and medicinal uses and were used in teas, conserves, and oils.

As a result of its popularity and as a symbol of civility and beauty, the rose was transported across the globe as a fine treasure. Damask roses were probably brought to Europe from the Middle East by the Crusaders. William Penn sailed with roses to America in 1699 only to find that the Indians already had transplanted wild roses as decorations for their encampments. The 'Sweet Briar' rose, *Rosa rubiginosa,* was introduced to Massachusetts by the Puritans. Early settlers packed 'Harison's Yellow' rose into Conestoga wagons for the trip westward on the Oregon Trail. In a dramatic story rivaling the plot of an espionage novel, budwood of the

'Peace' rose was smuggled out of France as the Germans invaded during World War II. As a fitting monument, 'Peace' was first presented to the United Nations delegation in 1945 to mark the end of the war.

The Cultivated Rose

The genealogy of the rose reveals no direct lineage because its ancestors hail from all over the globe above the equator (no species of rose evolved naturally below the equator). Roses are classified into a family called *Rosaceae.* The wild rose genus *Rosa* was found in Europe, Asia, the Middle East, and America. *Rosa* includes a variety of species roses that grow naturally in the wild and are the ancestors of all cultivars; if you plant a seed from a parent species rose, the offspring will be genetically the same as the parent. Roses such as *Rosa eglanteria,* the Eglantine rose, and other wild species roses generally are underused in gardens today.

Both nature and man succeeded in creating rose hybrids. The Dutch worked actively to create new strains through hybridization, the process of interbreeding two roses to create a new rose. Hybridization changed the history of roses forever because it gave breeders the ability to create roses with specific characteristics. By the end of the 18th century, rose breeding was greatly enhanced by the introduction of *Rosa chinensis,* the China rose, and *Rosa gigantea,* the tea rose, both from China, which infused several new rose traits, the most revolutionary being the trait of repeat flowering. By the late 19th century, there were large numbers of hybrids, some carefully engineered, and some created by chance. These new roses brought about a new class, the hybrid tea, which remains today the most popular bedding rose.

Although cultivated roses are defined by specific classes, such as albas, bourbons, mosses, damasks, and others, in general, roses fall into two categories: old roses, introduced before 1867, and

modern roses, introduced after. Old roses can be loosely described as having an open flower and are shrublike in structure. Modern roses exhibit larger budding blooms and stand upright. As a bedding and landscaping guide for roses, this book describes roses in the following categories:

Climbers and Ramblers

Climbers and ramblers are classified by their upward and outward growth. Climbers have long canes that can be tied to a support such as a trellis or wall. They generally produce large clusters of bloom. Some are called pillar roses. Smaller than other climbers, these roses can grow without support in an upright or "pillar" position. Ramblers have more supple canes than climbers and can be trained onto a fence or trellis. They bloom profusely once a season.

Shrub and Landscape Roses

Shrub and landscape roses produce beautiful blooms and require little maintenance. Shrub roses take various forms—tidy bushes with small clusters of flowers, tall arching plants, or ranging bushes that are ideal for hedges.

Old Garden Roses

Old garden roses are a large class made up of 10 groups of roses that have been cultivated since 1867. Any rose in a class before hybrid teas is an old garden rose. These voluptuous roses have flowers that usually are large, round, and very full. Some have as many as 200 petals per flower, and all have an exquisite fragrance. They have seen a resurgence in popularity since the mid-1950s.

Floribundas

Floribundas are hardy, low growing, and bushy. They have large blossoms that bloom singly or in clusters. Floribundas, a modern rose, were developed by crossbreeding hybrid teas with polyanthas, another modern rose. The result is sprays that are ever-blooming.

Hybrid Teas

Hybrid teas represent the classic image of the rose: a single bud on a long, elegant stem. The bud elegantly unfolds into a high-centered blossom. Regarded as the standard for bedding roses, the hybrid tea produces blooms in nearly all colors, and some varieties are known for their rich fragrance. The rose was introduced in 1867 as a cross between hybrid perpetuals and tea roses, and the hybridization took the best traits of both roses, resulting in a relatively short bush with a wide range of colors. The hybrid tea is the most popular rose today.

Grandifloras

Grandifloras inherited the best traits of their parents, the hybrid tea and the floribunda. From their hybrid tea lineage, grandifloras gained their flower form and long stem. The large, vigorous blooms are perfect for cutting. Their floribunda relative infused grandifloras with the ability to continually bloom. These hardy roses exceed both their parents in height, and therefore are excellent as a backdrop to other roses in a border or used alone as a hedge.

Miniatures

Miniature roses range from 3 to 18 inches in height and come in all colors. Small but hardy, miniature roses exhibit well-formed buds and are extremely free-flowering. Because miniature roses are grown on their own root stock, they are often more winter hardy than taller grafted roses like hybrid teas. These popular little roses are ideal for small gardens and containers and can even be grown indoors. Some miniature varieties are also available in climbing form and grow 3 to 5 feet tall.

2

Roses in Modern Gardens

From colorful cottage beds to formal plantings among the boxwood, what is lovelier than a rose garden in full bloom. For these dedicated gardeners, it's the ultimate reward. Step behind the picket fences and stroll beneath the arbors to enjoy their spectacular blooms and share their gardening secrets.

A Classic Mix

In Cathy Farmer's family tree, garden putterers abound.

"Both my grandmothers loved gardens," Cathy says. "My mother always had a few rosebushes, planted seeds in spring, and had a few tomatoes and vegetables. So I guess I'm fulfilling not only my dreams, but theirs, too, which is kind of a nice feeling," says Cathy, who is president of the Greater Atlanta Rose Society and lives in Woodstock, an Atlanta suburb.

"I must have picked up their feelings for flowers, particularly because I think of them often when I'm in my garden. That's one of the neat things about gardening. It's a really nice connected sort of feeling . . . to other people, to the earth. It's a very spiritual thing for me. I wish my grandmothers could see this garden because they would love it so much."

After several moves, this once-frustrated gardener and her family finally put down roots in their surburban home 12 years ago. The first year, Cathy planted 40 roses.

Although roses old and new are her passion, Cathy is an admitted "greedy gardener" who has tucked a dazzling mix of flowers into her home's ¾-acre lot. She has about 150 roses, including hybrid teas, floribundas, miniatures, modern shrubs, old garden varieties, and climbers, with few duplications. In the front yard, Cathy uses old garden and modern shrub roses as a landscaping device, with about 50 plants mixed single-file into graceful hedges 6 to 10 feet tall bordering both sides of the yard.

"When they're all in bloom, it's a fairly fabulous sight," Cathy says. "And when 'Rosa Mundi' is in bloom, I can hardly stay in the house . . . it's just lovely."

Old garden varieties, such as 'Rosa Mundi,' are among Cathy's favorites, and she has won Dowager Queen awards for two of her old roses at local and district American Rose Society-sanctioned shows. "On 'Rosa Mundi,' no two blooms are alike . . . . They're unevenly striped, or they have splashes of pink, deep pink, or almost red, on a white background. When it's in full bloom, it may have 200 to 300 blooms on it, and it's just an eye-popper," she says.

Other vintage favorites include 'Souvenir de la Malmaison,' a pale-pink bourbon prize of French Empress Josephine, and 'Etoile de Hollande,' a prolific and fragrant climber that, to Cathy, epitomizes the perfect red rose. Although roses are tucked "here, there, and everywhere" around her yard, she tunes into the plants' needs when picking sites. Clambering over a holly bush, tender roses that need wind protection are cast as foundation plants in a garden tucked into the home's south-facing ell. Four large climbers meander up wire trellises on the side of the house. In mixed beds, she carefully chooses perennials—Siberian and bearded iris, phlox, peonies, daylilies, sweet William, dianthus, and larkspur among others–to complement her roses.

Bordered by woods, the backyard has multiple gardens for flowers and vegetables, but the decided star is a 25x60-foot traditional bed filled with modern roses. She doesn't hesitate to move plants, even roses, for more artistic groupings of color and foliage. "I grow pretty much one of each. I have a few hybrid teas that I really like and I have two bushes, but that's the most duplicates I have," says Cathy, who counts fragrance, color, bloom form, and overall charisma among her criteria for selecting roses.

Cathy's husband Duane, a marriage and family therapist, is the lawn specialist on this gardening team, tending the stretches of green that frame the colorful beds. "Some rose people . . . plant the

Among the sparkling white 'Pascale' and fragrant 'Apricot Nectar' in her traditional rose bed, opposite, Cathy Farmer, above, tucks in perennials for color and stem camouflage.

whole lawn in roses, but I like to keep some grass because it looks pretty. It really sets off the flowers," she says.

"I like to try new things . . . a lot of good roses are still being discovered. I love all my roses, and they're all beautiful. But there's a special charm, a certain beauty I'm looking for, so I try new things looking for that. It's an emotional reaction to the flower. It's very personal."

Cathy's toughest challenges as a rose grower are the red Georgia clay and hot weather. "Roses don't mind a little clay, but they don't grow well in pure clay. So I dig all that soil out, mix it up with organic matter and sand, and replant in a much lighter soil mixture," Cathy says. In summer, when heat is intense and may be accompanied by drought, Cathy switches exclusively to liquid fertilizers "because the roses need extra water anyway, and the liquid fertilizer gives them a little boost, but it doesn't force them into heavy growth during that heat. Nobody likes to work too hard when it's really hot. It's not good for us, and it's not good for the roses either," she says.

To keep the roses free of diseases such as black spot, Cathy sprays weekly, in the cool, early morning hours, with a combination of two fungicides. She doesn't use an insecticide regularly, only when she sees problem insects. She fertilizes at least monthly through the growing season, and twice a month if there is time. Cathy also deadheads spent blooms to keep her roses producing into late fall, when cool nights and dry, sunny days bring on flowers that rival the initial spring flush.

For Cathy, gardening is more than a labor of love. It's a gift she's compelled to share. "It's a form of immortality," Cathy says. "I hope my daughters will be interested in gardening in their own way."

Spiky pink foxglove rises majestically from the crescent-shape border of perennials, left, that Cathy designed at the back of the yard. Including requisite roses and an oasis for birds and other thirsty critters, the plantings provide seemingly endless color against the woodland backdrop .

Seaside Blooms

For "30-something" years, Bob Levenson has been growing roses in gardens big and small. "I think the reason one plants roses is, aside from the obvious challenge, they look beautiful and they smell good," says Bob. "They behave in mysterious ways . . . but they are an accomplishment when you get them right."

In a mere three years, this retired advertising executive has transformed the backyard of the East Hampton, New York, home he shares with his wife Kathe Tanous, a professional artist, into a fragrant oasis.

A few aged crab apple trees were the extent of backyard flora when the couple moved in and began renovating the home and grounds. Today those trees have colorful company in beautifully designed gardens, poolside berms with perennial borders, and structural plantings—all featuring roses. Even two of the apple trees now have 'May Queen' climbers entwined among the branches.

Although his rose collection embraces about 100 varieties and includes every type of rose from antique plants to modern hybrids, one of the yard's showstoppers is his "ginkzebo," an arbor with ginkgo trees forming the structure and 'Rosa soulieana' climbers spreading thousands of tiny white blossoms up the sides and over the canopy, about 15 feet high. It makes an especially inviting spot to linger on a warm summer's day.

Bob also has a more traditional roses-only bed, a 20x70-foot plot he has dubbed the "rose department." There's a grass path for browsers and even a touch of his wry humor—an old door scavenged from a demolished house. Hung at the yew hedge bordering the rose garden, this architectural artifact is planted with 'New Dawn,' a prolific, pale pink climber. "It sort of looks like you

can walk through it, like the door is going through the hedge, but it doesn't go anyplace," he says.

By design, Bob's roses-only bed leans toward the wild side because he likes to let his plants "bump into each other." He maintains the upper hand, however, carefully orchestrating symmetry in color and asymmetry in scale. "For a long time, when I gardened in other places, I tried to segregate roses by color, by form, the French textbook way of doing it. The roses were sort of controlling me. I like it better when I control them," he explains.

Working on instinct and expertise, Bob has a knack for displaying roses to their best advantage, capitalizing on attributes, whether it be color, form, or growing habit. He uses 'Nozomi' as ground cover for a blanket of pale pink blossoms. In a rose garden experiment, 'Compassion,' a pink-and-yellow climber, becomes a lush bush because he persuaded it not to climb. Thornless 'Fantin-Latour,' with deep pink blooms, and fragrant 'Queen Elizabeth' perfume a bedroom thanks to prevailing southerly winds.

"'Queen Elizabeth' is close to cast iron," Bob says. "It's not a quitter. It just keeps on producing all summer long. Everybody should love it. It should be mandatory. It's a nice rose to grow here, there, and everywhere,"

Some roses are underplanted with roses or repeating daylilies for color between blooms. On berms around the pool house he has used tree and low-growing varieties of 'The Fairy' together. "Anything that produces color on a continuing basis is my friend," he adds. Another favorite is 'Pristine,' a white rose tinged with pale pink that he likes to plant among the peonies.

Bob honed his green thumb on his own. "Actually this is probably a reaction on my part to any kind of gardening, the fact that we didn't have a garden," he says of his childhood. "I like to be

Roses meander almost everywhere in the backyard retreat of gardener Bob Levenson and his wife Kathe Tanous, above. An earthen berm is planted in roses and perennials, opposite. The trellises mark the entrance to the "rose department."

'Compassion,' a climber with varied pink-and-yellow blossoms, above, rambles over a fence near the swimming pool. The "ginkzebo," left, is a fragrant spot for relaxing and catching sea breezes. Bob created the "ginkzebo" from ginkgo trees and climbing roses.

outside, and I don't mind getting my hands dirty. The reward is enormous, and I can say 'Look Ma, I did that,' or at least I didn't get in its way."

When the forsythia blooms, that's Bob's cue to start spring pruning. He treats each plant to a helping of his "witch's brew," a concoction that includes epsom salts, alfalfa meal, a mix of commercial and organic fertilizers such as bat guano or earthworm castings, and composted manure.

Although the temperate seaside climate indulges gardeners, losing plants is inevitable and he gives roses a couple of years to prove themselves. "Some make it, some don't," Bob says. "You lose a certain number of bushes no matter what you do."

When he was designing the gardens, Bob was tempted to hire a professional "but I made a conscious decision to do it myself this time," he says. "In the past, we've had some very good people who taught me a lot, but it turned out to be their garden. This is a very personal garden. I get the best compliments from professional landscape people who take the garden tours."

Country Airs

It's an idyllic slice of Midwest Americana—tree-lined streets, past-perfect homes, manicured lawns, and sidewalks alive with walkers, joggers, and children on bicycles. It's the kind of setting that has long inspired artists and authors, and today inspires rose gardener Marla Bouchein.

Once fields and meadows stretched beyond her 1861 colonial-style farmhouse. Now, nestled behind a charming white picket fence on a spacious corner lot, it's one of many landmark homes in Kirkwood, Missouri, a St. Louis suburb. It's Marla's colorful country garden of floribundas, grandifloras, hybrid teas, and climbers, however, that has turned her home into a showstopper.

"There's a lot of traffic past my garden," Marla says. "It's fun to look out and see people standing there peeking over the fence, asking how much longer before the roses bloom, or just enjoying the flowers. Even people with cameras, asking if they may take photos. This garden gives so much pleasure."

A former registered nurse, Marla and her husband Dave count the home's big yard, the rich soil, and the gardening time they spend together among life's luxuries. "It's a wonderful hobby," she says. "I'd rather be in the dirt than anywhere else. There's a kind of common language with gardening, and flowers are a connection for people."

Marla inherited her love of flowers in general, and roses in particular, from her father, who was an avid gardener, and from her German grandfather, who had a background in horticulture. "So in my family, I just saw generations that did something with roses, and I guess I've always had a love for them," she says. "They're the queen of all flowers."

When Marla and Dave purchased the house, what now is the rose garden was merely a concrete aggregate pathway and a couple of rosebushes. Marla's vision and green thumb turned the barely begun dream of a former owner into reality. She has 34 varieties in one rose bed, plus two climbers on the same side of the house. An ever-blooming 'America,' in a peachy-apricot color, rambles over the picket fence, adding to the cottage garden appeal. But Marla is working on a dream of her own, incorporating antique roses somewhere on the property.

Marla selects roses for their beauty, hardiness, and fragrance. "It's just my way of expressing myself," she says. Fragrance is an important factor in her selections, because "it's not only beauty, you want to put your nose down and smell them." One favorite is 'Double Delight,' a fragrant tea rose with a variegated yellowy bloom that goes to pink. But peach- and apricot-hued roses are her favorites, and when she does bouquets, she adds 'French Lace,' a creamy white floribunda, and 'John F. Kennedy,' a dazzling white hybrid tea.

In planning her nostalgic roses-only bed, one of several garden spots in the yard, Marla researched specialty rose growers' catalogs to create the perfect mix of colors, heights and foliage. "I usually purchase by mail order and plant roses when they are dormant, so I'm seeing no green on them. I put them in in March as soon as the soil is workable and the growers can ship," she says. "I just remember my grandfather did this. I feel like maybe your plants get a good start right where they're going to be. I don't know that I've ever put a rose in here in bud."

To say that the area's climate—"cooker summers" and winter temperatures that often hover near zero—are unkind to gardeners is an understatement. "I think you've got to be very patient," Marla

Marla Bouchein, above, planted 'America' along her picket fence. The magnificent rose garden in her side yard, opposite, stops passersby. They often ask to take photographs.

says. "I've had years when things have not gone well. Each spring if it's been a hard winter, I've had to say I'm going to lose plants. You have to expect that. Even though roses are a long-lived perennial, you will lose them if diseases attack and you're not aware, or maybe if you've had a very hard winter and it was not a healthy plant going into winter. We work hard so we can see what we have from May to October. It's trial and error, and I think that keeps your creative interest. If something didn't work this year, you can try a new avenue, or a fellow gardener is going to tell you a new secret."

"I think the secret with roses is that you should keep on cutting, because the more you cut, the more they're going to bloom," she says. "Cut your roses. Bring them in. I love to have them out there in the garden, but I love to have them inside, too."

Marla understands why some gardeners hesitate to grow roses, but urges them to give it a try. "They think they're something special, and I think the special part is you have to be a little more attuned to what they need. Roses do have a care factor. You just have to love them enough to want to care for them," she says.

Because it's visible from the street, the rose garden draws appreciative crowds. It's not the only garden in Marla's yard, however. A big fan of perennials, she starts her own seedlings in flats inside, and fills beds with peonies, clematis, yarrow, phlox, daylilies, and veronica, tucking high-color annuals in between. Zinnias are a favorite staple because they attract butterflies. In the backyard, there's a woodland garden of hostas and ferns and a Japanese garden with a fish pond.

"Gardening, especially roses, is a wonderful, creative outlet for me," Marla says. "Seeing the pleasure our garden gives others makes me want to go out and do more because I know how much people enjoy it."

Marla has 34 varieties of roses in her country-style garden, opposite, including the pink 'Queen Elizabeth,' top left. She doesn't hesitate to mix hybrid teas, grandifloras, and floribundas in a rainbow of colors, bottom left.

Secret Garden

In the lush suburban wonderland of Dee and Chris Gronbeck, Alice of storybook fame would feel quite at home because their well-tended roses grow to surprising size.

Beyond the rose-edged entry courtyard that's a delight in itself, bushy floribundas and hybrid teas tower overhead, wooden arbors and trellises are laden with showy, long-stemmed beauties, and, from late spring on, thousands of blooms turn the yard of their Kentfield, California, home, near San Francisco, into a fragrant fantasy of color.

"It's like being in a secret garden," says Dee, who acknowledges that nurturing the couple's varied collection of roses brings out her maternal instincts. "I have a 'Queen Elizabeth' rose. I don't know what height it's supposed to be, but it's growing above the top of the greenhouse off the bedroom. It's almost to the second story."

The Gronbecks' individual talents complement each other and add up to gardening success. Dee, who used to put brush to canvas, has the artist's eye when it comes to choosing and mixing roses, perennials, and native plants for color, texture, and foliage. Chris, a retired physician, keeps the roses "on the straight and narrow" by following a meticulous care schedule.

Eschewing the disciplines of more formal gardens, the Gronbecks instead celebrate their roses' naturally willful ways. By allowing the bushy plants to go vertical, some 8 to 10 feet tall, they make the most of their yard and are able to pack more roses among the extensive plantings on their quarter-acre lot.

Although the Gronbeck garden is filled with a mostly modern mix of roses, Dee insists that it's not a rose garden. "It's a garden with roses in it," she says. "Some people plant roses by themselves, very formal and wonderful, but that's not what we wanted. We have roses among our perennial plants and roses among our native plants. We went up because we didn't have anywhere else to go on the level . . . everything was chock-a-block full."

Like the house, built in the early 1960s, the gardens have evolved over three decades as Chris and Dee honed their gardening skills and experimented to find their favorites. Not wanting to miss a minute of the glorious show of blooms, the couple designed decks, trellises, and arbors to frame the wraparound garden views. Because the house is at a different level than the pool and main garden, plantings intentionally camouflage gradual changes in ground level. One of Dee's favorite roses, 'Peace,' mingles with trumpet vine clytostoma on an arbor and with xylosma, nicotiana, flax, iris, and cranesbill geraniums in the bed underscoring the deck. 'First Prize' meanders over another deck arbor.

When it comes to the garden's palette, Dee's tastes run to 'Brandy,' 'Just Joey,' 'Peace,' and 'Golden Showers,' and to coppery tones that go well with pinks, such as 'Seashell,' mixed with creams and whites. She's not a fan of traditional red roses that have blue undertones, which she says tend to fade in California's hot, sunny conditions.

Because the gardens continue to be artistic works-in-progress, the Gronbecks occasionally can't resist experimenting with different varieties. New additions from local nurseries and specialty rose growers may arrive, but they soon go if they don't perform. "It's trial and error," Dee says. "I've made a thousand mistakes." Currently she is searching for 'Silver Jubilee,' a pink-and-brown mix she discovered in a friend's garden.

Roses also are popping up in other yards around the Gronbecks' neighborhood, because if a specific rose doesn't fit into their garden

Masses of blooms, opposite, envelop the California home of gardeners Dee and Chris Gronbeck, above, in a riot of color and fragrance.

scheme, they pass it along and let other gardeners try their hand with it. "I've had rosebushes I decided I didn't like, and flowers that were too hard to bother with, or didn't show enough." Dee says.

Roses demand a commitment, but the Gronbecks believe the rewards are worth it. Patience, discipline, and "a thick skin" to withstand thorny toils are requisites, too. "You have to have a routine," Dee says. "My husband's a good pruner and he does the feeding and spraying. He does the work, and I do the flower arranging and the planning of what goes where, the colors, and all that."

Because they did not take up gardening until they retired, the Gronbecks are convinced that gardeners are made not born. "There are no secrets," Chris says. "What we're doing is sort of straightforward, just following directions."

With several dozen rose varieties blooming nearly nonstop throughout the year, it's not surprising that the Gronbeck home and their friends' homes are filled with Dee's flower arrangements. Even as she cuts blooms, Dee continues to shape the plants by carefully selecting which branches to snip. And, as the couple walks through the gardens, it's become second nature to snip off dead blooms, yank wayward weeds, and check for white fly.

Alone, in classic arrangements, or combined with other flowers, roses are Dee's artistic medium. She especially likes mixing roses with native grasses. "You know everybody's a frustrated artist," she says. "I think you'll find most people have some talent for mixing garden colors, textures, and foliage. If they garden for any length of time, they will."

The Gronbecks have made the most of their ¼ acre of suburban land, incorporating a wide variety of plants, with roses predominating. Bushy floribundas and hybrid teas tower overhead, and wooden arbors and trellises are laden with showy, long-stem beauties, transforming their home into a fragrant fantasy of color.

Artful Approach

For gardener Arlene Wolf, capturing the perfect palette has been the inspiration for the exquisite gardens of roses, perennials, and woodland plants that she has created around her Long Island, New York, home.

"Monet's garden is the perfect example of color—when you see it in photographs, it looks like a hundred acres. It's not. That's what makes it so brilliant," says Arlene, who brings home many ideas from her travels for her own seaside gardens. "I realized the whole point of growing flowers is to play with the color."

Arlene's gardens very much resemble a small botanic garden. She has a woodland garden, a rock garden, a perennial garden, and an architectural garden. "The reason I wound up with roses, aside from the fact that I've always loved them and always had a couple, was they are the most versatile flower for color," she says.

The expansive back lawn, bordered by trees, slopes down to wetlands and the sea, making a tranquil blue-green foil for the rose beds bursting with summer color. For the home's entry, Arlene sought a more formal mood, with roses tucked into manicured boxwood. Arlene turned her wish list over to landscape architect Naniko Umberto, who created personalized plots to tame the space.

"What I needed was a place to do all the different plants I'm interested in, and she was brilliant," Arlene says. "She defined the space as a little botanic garden. She came up with the concept of the crescents and the hedgerows, and she created different spaces where I could do my horticultural thing."

Design mandates included keeping the woodland areas, now set off by hedgerows, as natural as possible and creating architecturally interesting gardens in the sun for Arlene's colorful experiments. After four days spent working with the bulldozing crew that was reshaping the site, Arlene had her dream spaces, including five 12x24-foot crescent-shape beds for roses on the sloping back lawn.

"What I was able to achieve with all these different areas was color 12 months a year," Arlene says. "Even in winter, in February, I have heather that blooms in the rock garden. It's only two little pieces, but it's a little bit of purple."

After the layout was completed, Arlene chose the plantings, poring over international gardening catalogs. She selected an assortment of mostly modern hybrid roses strictly on color, with fragrance her second criterion. Some plants didn't thrive in the climate and had to be replaced. Some surprised her by exceeding the typical growing pattern in height, necessitating changes to maintain the tiers of color.

Hardy rugosa varieties—"seaside plants," she calls them—have been among the star performers in her "very eclectic collection" of approximately 350 roses. The collection includes climbers, tree roses, teas, and new English shrubs that have a full, old-fashioned look in the blooms that repeat throughout the season. "It's whatever rose would survive with the color that I needed," she says.

Nowhere is Arlene's color philosophy more beautifully apparent than in the roses-only crescent beds. One bed holds deep reds and maroons; another, maroons, deep pinks, and pale pinks; and others, yellows and whites; buffs, pinks, and oranges; and clear reds and lavenders. Beginning in early June, the crescent gardens delight with "a month's worth of wonderful flowers," then repeat with a second flush in mid-August.

Trees, hedgerows, and wetlands, opposite, serve as a backdrop for rose beds in the backyard of Arlene Wolf, above. Five crescent-shape rose beds are planted on the sloping back lawn of her Long Island, New York, home. Arlene designs her gardens according to color.

Arlene's collection of 350 roses includes climbers, tree roses, teas, and English shrubs, left and above. Rugosa varieties have been the star performers in her seaside locale. The rose gardens bloom for about a month in early summer, then a second wave of color appears in mid-August.

The key to successful rose growing, Arlene says, is experimenting to find the varieties that thrive in a specific climate. In her seaside location, hybrids have rewarded her efforts. Among her favorites are the creamy pink 'Queen Elizabeth,' "a very lush bush that seems to be in bloom forever"; 'Bonica,' which "you can plant in cement"; 'Medallion,' a pale apricot tea; and the reliable 'Peace' and comely 'Garden Party.' Her favorite rose is 'Pristine.' "It's a very pale, ivory bud, and when it opens up, it's a blushy pink with a deeper pink fringe around the flower. When the light comes through it, it really looks like a piece of porcelain," she says. "It's not particularly prolific, but it holds its shape very well, and as a single flower, it's absolutely exquisite."

The response to the gardens from friends and garden tourists has been wonderful, Arlene says. "Everybody loves it. It's very restful." In warm weather, the yard with an ocean view is a natural for home entertaining, and garden party guests are invited to stroll among the rose crescents and through her other personality gardens before dinner.

English Accent

Up Sonoma Mountain, nestled in the lupine-covered hills and redwood groves near Santa Rosa, California, there's a fragrant bit of England, where roses tumble over the pergola, ramble up the barn, and mingle everywhere in a changing tapestry of perennials.

It's a colorful composite of half-overgrown country gardens that delighted British-born garden designer Michael Bates as a child. His love of roses is rooted in those classic English gardens, where he always discovered new things. For the setting of his turn-of-the-century home, he'd settle for nothing less.

"I grew up gardening. Basically, I was taught gardening by my mother, as I think most people probably are," says Michael, who views roses as one of the most endearing features of English gardens because they are equally at home climbing a farmhouse porch or tucked among the formal boxwood of a grand manor house. "My greatest satisfaction is when English friends come to visit, they say, 'It's nice to see a real garden.'"

Considering what Michael and his wife Helen encountered on their first visit to the property over a decade ago, the transformation is, indeed, miraculous. The wood-frame house was run-down and surrounded by a mostly asphalt lawn, a chain-link fence, and a few overgrown camellia bushes. But in the property, the couple saw not only room to grow but the serenity that had eluded them in the city.

Reviving the house and gardens simultaneously proved too time-consuming, so the Bates' hired someone to finish the house and they focused on the gardens. For starters, they had to haul out seven truck loads of rocks and haul in seven loads of cow manure.

For Michael, highly skilled in horticulture and design, bringing home the first rosebushes was like a reunion with old friends, and, as the gardens have evolved over the years, so has his career. Today his thriving English Country Gardens firm designs lush landscapes for a variety of clients, including estates and wineries.

"One of the things my gardens have taught me is what I can and can't hope to use in other people's gardens," Michael explains. "I'm sitting down here with a plan, and I often jump up and go outside with a tape measure and actually measure plants. My plotting plans are done to scale, so my gardens are a true working laboratory in that sense."

In his personal gardens, Michael marries past and present with complementary plantings of antique roses and a mix of modern hybrids, which offer continuous flowering and color variety. "I think the rose has an enduring allure in the sense that it's both a flower of nostalgia and a flower of history. It's an amazing plant. I can't think of another plant like the rose that really stamps its style on gardens quite as much," he says.

With an artist's eye and instinct, Michael creates signature environments for his roses, using them as structural plantings on trellises, arbors, and fences; as accents; and in cutting gardens and borders mixed with perennials and native grasses. He prefers the blousy, untamed look in his blooms and allows roses to amble almost at will. In the distinctive borders, for example, he combines shrub roses such as 'Penelope' and 'Autumn Delight' and hybrid teas such as 'Lady Hillingdon' with columbines, irises, peonies, and hardy geraniums, among other perennials.

"I like mixing plants and creating a tapestry of color." Michael says. "I like plants growing through other plants, such as the iris coming up through the lamb's-ear, even though it looks like an

Michael Bates, above, stands under one of his arbors that is covered with roses all summer long. Opposite, graceful sprays of 'Fortune's Double Yellow' appear in April.

unmade bed. The garden looks nice all summer even if things are not blooming because there is a happy conjunction of shapes and forms and textures. I try to achieve a mix of perennials, but the roses keep making up their own minds."

Tiers of plants create layered palettes of color. Michael has been patient in composing the garden through the years. If a certain rose fails to thrive, he unsentimentally replaces it. He has grown some roses in 7-gallon pots in the garden for a year to test their hardiness and performance, and if they pass they join the permanent plantings.

"The ones that you tend to fall out of love with pretty quickly are the ones you have to spend your life spraying and pruning," he says. "It's too much work. That's a speedy disenchantment."

Although lawns in the West fell into some disfavor during recent drought years, "flat levels of calm," such as stretches of grass, are imperative for truly beautiful gardens," Michael says. His gravel driveway between border gardens and a flagstone path in the yard serve this purpose.

Today Michael practices restraint in his rose plantings and diversity in gardens not only for endless color but also to guard against diseases that could wipe out a roses-only bed. "Now I don't add as much as I edit. I don't want to be only a rose gardener," says Michael, who subtracts several roses each year. "I can't imagine either designing or owning a garden without roses. It's just that you have to find a balance for them because they're probably one of the most time-consuming of all plants."

Michael understands that many home gardeners think they have to plant every inch of yard space. He has run out of room, too. "What you learn is that sometimes you need to edit, you need to take things out. The voids become as important as the solids to create the energy in the space," he says.

A lush green lawn helps set the stage for extraordinary flower borders filled with perennials and roses.

3

Roses in the Landscape

The rose is a testament to man's creativity; once a wild flower, the rose has been cultivated and engineered to suit the needs of all types of gardens and landscapes. Whether growing on a rocky wall, cascading over an arbor, blooming in a container, or growing in a formal garden devoted entirely to themselves, roses will transform any setting into a festival of flowers.

Roses in Your Front Yard

First impressions count. That's why roses are so valuable for front-yard gardens. They can be the single key to transforming your entry into an inviting passageway laden with bloom and fragrance. Roses are not the primma donnas many people make them out to be. There's a host of colorful, yet tough new hybrids available that will work as well by your front door as they would in a traditional formal garden.

For your front-yard roses to excel, you must consider their environmental requirements. Actually, roses are fairly tolerant of most conditions, but they do require at least six hours of sunlight per day and should be planted away from shrubs or trees, which will compete for light, water, and soil nutrients. The sunniest, southern exposure is excellent for roses. If you plant roses next to the foundation of your house, make sure they receive adequate water because overhanging eaves and gutter systems can keep them from receiving rainfall. The soil in which you plant roses also is vital to their success. Some roses may thrive in poor soils but others will not, so consult your local nursery or garden center to determine the proper soil amendments to help your roses become hardy producers.

Before planting, take an inventory of your front yard, noting locations that could benefit from an added dose of color. Look for any open, sunny spot that you may not have considered before. Here are some planting ideas to keep in mind as you tour your landscape.

Any front yard or entry can be dressed up by climbers and ramblers. For a casual look, plant 'Aloha' on a weather-worn fence where its 3- to 5-inch double pink blooms and bright yellow stamens will show. On a white fence, the elegant crimson, cupped blooms of 'Blaze' catch fire when their buds open. Sunny clusters of 'Golden Showers' cascading over the top of a doorway say welcome to visitors.

A mass of low-growing floribundas, such as 'Sweet Inspiration' or 'Betty Prior,' require little care while producing large patches of sustained color for your yard. Use them in beds in front of your house or in a sunny side yard to disguise an unattractive foundation. Another way to use floribundas is to team them with flowering shrubs or perennials for an all-season color show. The floribundas remain colorful all summer long, while the shrubs and perennials go in and out of bloom. Floribundas work well in a border or as an edging along property lines. They also make an effective and beautiful plant to line a walkway to your front door.

Grandifloras are large enough to plant as property dividers, front hedges, or screens and may even eliminate the need for a less attractive privacy structure or fence. Planted as a hedge a grandiflora such as 'Love' produces continuous clusters of red and white hybrid-tea-form blooms. The elegant pink blooms of the towering 'Queen Elizabeth' make a living privacy screen at your property's edge. Grandifloras also are excellent bedding plants, but because of their height they are best placed in back-of-the-border positions.

A curbside bed of hybrid teas brightens this yard and provides armloads of fragrant cut flowers all season.

This wrought-iron fence is enhanced with the exuberant trusses of a red climber.

Some varieties of shrub and landscape roses are low growing and can cover a slope or hillside. These persistent and hardy roses send out long shoots that allow the rose to spread horizontally very quickly. An added feature, and one to consider when selecting landscaping plants, is their ability to fill beds with bloom quickly, eliminating the need to weed.

'Sea Foam' or 'White Meidiland' make excellent ground covers. Consider planting them in locations where their long ground-hugging canes can tumble over rock wall or terraces. Shrub and landscape roses also come in taller, dense varieties that make good hedges, such as 'White Simplicity' and 'Fair Bianca.' If you want to camouflage an unsightly view, a hedge of roses is a colorful solution to your problem.

For small gardens or for scattered bursts of color, choose miniature roses. These robust little bloomers won't overstep their

Pink roses and perennial flowers stage a classic white fence with bloom.

space, but provide a never-ending supply of tiny, well-formed flowers that are also fine for cutting. Planted along your front walk, these stocky little troopers stand and deliver bloom with great consistency in color and shape. In a rock garden, pop in a miniature or two to add color where needed. Or consider a border of colorful miniatures in front of an evergreen foundation planting.

Landscaping a New Home

Landscaping a new home allows you more flexibility in planting roses. Before you break ground and drop in your first rose, plan how roses will enhance your entryway and front-yard. Be sure to consider the overall style of your home before you plant, however. Evaluate the entry and list its architectural components such as walkways, fences, porches, pergolas, arbors, archways, and trellises. Your front yard landscaping should enhance, not overpower, the basic design of your home.

The sheer number of rose varieties to choose from may seem a bit intimidating at first, so doing a bit of research may be helpful. After determining which roses you like based on color and plant characteristics, verify with a local nursery or garden center that they are winter hardy for your zone. A good way to witness roses that are hardy in your area is to survey the roses in your neighborhood or in a local horticultural garden or park. Also refer to books and the good advice of rose gardeners in your area.

Once you've decided which roses you want to plant, consider how they will harmonize together. Planting one rose of each color may produce a discordant effect, so settle on a color scheme. Red, white, and pink roses blend nicely, as do apricot and yellow roses.

Choosing Colors

When selecting a rose color, also consider how the roses will look with the color of your home. White roses planted against a white house may not be discernable from their background. Roses are most dramatic when planted against a backdrop that allows their blooms to take center stage. Excellent varieties of red roses are

Blooming drifts of grandifloras, florabundas, and hybrid teas add color and elegance along this brick driveway.

'Dortmund,' 'Chrysler Imperial,' and 'Mister Lincoln.' For a selection of white roses, plant 'Iceberg,' 'Honor,' 'Pascali,' and 'Sea Foam.' Pink roses include 'First Prize,' 'Grüss an Aachen,' and 'The Fairy.' For subtle mauves, try 'Lavender Lace' and 'Angel Face.' Coral or apricot roses are best represented by 'Mojave,' 'Brandy,' and 'Medallion.' Yellow roses such as 'Golden Showers,' 'Maréchal Niel,' and 'Lawrence Johnston' are reliable choices.

Evaluate how the roses you've selected will interact with the existing plants in your front entryway. Keep in mind the growth limitations of some roses in northern climates. Although winter hardy, a rose may not grow as large as it could in a more temperate climate. If you want a rose climbing above your doorway, plant a winter-hardy climbing variety and double up with a perennial such as clematis.

Roses also can cast an inviting fragrance. Imagine the delight of a visitor who is met with the bright red blooms of 'Crimson Glory' and its rich rose fragrance. Plant some by the front door so that you can enjoy their perfume whenever you return home or step outdoors. Many bedding varieties exude a rich scent: For a red and yellow bloom with extraordinary fragrance, plant 'Double Delight'; the bright gold 'Oregold' exhibits a light fruity scent; and the medium pink 'Perfume Delight' provides a memorable fragrance.

Roses teamed with perennials such as peony, Siberian iris, cranesbill geranium, allium, and artemisia create a traffic-stopping display of bloom.

49

Roses in Containers

Portable roses are an effective way to enhance your outdoor living space, to change the look of your landscape, or to add color and beauty to your environment, especially when time or space is in short supply.

For a movable feast of color, position roses in containers where flower color is needed most. Dress up your deck, patio, or balcony with a bright collection of roses in pots and planters. Even window boxes or hanging baskets will accommodate some rose varieties. In fact, many roses flourish as well in containers as they do in the ground, providing they have ample sun, water, and occasional feedings. From stocky miniature roses in pots descending a stairway to whiskey barrel planters overflowing with rangy floribundas, there's a wide selection of roses for container gardens.

When space or time is limited, roses planted in containers offer bright spots of color in exchange for a minimal amount of care. Containers of roses can beautify a city balcony or rooftop as easily as they can enhance a suburban patio or deck. And unlike traditional rose gardens, containers make a simple task of moving roses around for a change of scene.

Container Roses

Nearly all roses, with the possible exception of large climbers and ramblers, do well in containers. Miniatures and smaller hybrid teas and floribundas do particularly well in containers. Miniatures have the added bonus of growing equally well indoors as out. Set on a sunny windowsill or under grow lights, miniatures will continue to bloom long after frost has withered the roses outside. Several popular miniature rose varieties are 'Baby Betsy McCall,' 'Julie Ann,' and 'Galaxy.'

Miniatures with a spreading growth habit, such as 'Green Ice,' 'Lavender Jewel,' and 'Stars 'n' Stripes,' are ideal for hanging baskets and window boxes. These hardy and prolific bloomers can brighten a front porch or overhang, and thrive in hanging baskets or on lampposts or porch overhangs. The red blooms of 'Kathy'

planted alongside corresponding annuals like dusty-miller and asparagus fern make a lovely window box combination. Or try the snow white blooms of 'Popcorn' mixed with the rich blue flowers of lobelia for a blue and white color scheme.

For more dramatic containers, use larger roses such as hybrid teas and floribundas. Buy budded plants from your local nursery or garden center, pot them up, and move them to a patio or deck for an instant rose garden. Hybrid teas make elegant single specimens upright and branching from a container. Select smaller hybrid teas such as 'Peace,' 'Perfume Delight,' and 'Whiskey Mac' for containers. A bushy variety, such as 'The Fairy,' cascades with blooms down the sides of any container. Other roses that excel in pots are 'Ballerina,' 'Cécile Brünner,' 'Jacques Cartier,' and 'Grüss an Aachen.'

Standard or tree roses (either full size or miniature), transplanted into a pot exude a formal air when paired at an entryway. Increase their color by planting a complementary annual in the pot with the tree rose. Flowering or scented geraniums are good choices. Or contrast the upright growth of a standard rose by planting a trailing annual such as petunias or lantana underneath.

Choosing a Container

Nearly any container will accommodate a standard-size rose if it's at least 18 inches across and deep and has adequate drainage. Miniatures will survive in smaller pots. Any type of pot will work as long as it has adequate drainage holes in the bottom. Terra-cotta, plastic, wood, or ceramic planters all create different looks for the roses they contain.

If you live in a northern climate where roses frequently have trouble overwintering, you may want to move your roses to a more sheltered location at the end of summer, so select a container accordingly. For this purpose, plastic containers are lightweight and

Set a container of 'The Fairy' tableside for instant outdoor dining color.

can be moved easily. They also won't crack like terra-cotta or ceramic pots if they are left out in the elements over the winter. For larger roses, however, plastic pots may be too light, causing your roses to topple in a strong wind. To solve the problem, simply fasten casters to the base of your larger pots so you can move them easily.

Container Style

Pots and planters should correspond to the style of your home's exterior. The container you choose can dress up or dress down the rose it holds. For example, a white wooden planter box with decorative finials planted with a standard tree rose would be a fine choice for a traditional-style home. A rustic cedar box planted with 'French Lace' rose cascading with its clustered blooms would be at home in a country setting. The roses you select and their color and bloom form should be considered when choosing a container.

Care for Container Roses

Choose a spot for containers where the roses will receive at least six hours of sunshine a day, the same as their cousins planted in traditional beds. When planting roses, use a potting soil mixture with a high content of Canadian sphagnum peat moss to retain water.

Because container roses are exposed to winds and sun, they dry out much faster than other roses. It's important to water them before they become bone-dry. During dry spells, be sure to water container roses every day. On extremely hot days, you may want to move your roses out of the strong midday sun. A good water-soluble fertilizer once a month will keep your roses in top shape.

In cold climates, move the planters indoors or to an unheated porch, garage, or basement. Containers also may be sunk in the ground or placed in a cold frame. Check periodically to make sure the medium is moist.

Standard roses combined in pots with other roses and annuals create a linear garden that leads you down the patio walkway.

Roses Overhead

Raise your garden to new heights by growing roses up and over a trellis, arbor, pergola, pillar, fence, or wall. All these structures provide support for a climber or rambler while offering valuable architectural interest to your home. Embellished with roses, these structures can even become the focal point in your garden.

Many varieties of roses are suitable for growing on structures, although somewhat fewer are reliably winter hardy in northern climates. 'American Pillar,' 'Dortmund,' 'Blaze Improved,' and several others will brave harsh winters. (See Chapter 4, "Portfolio of Roses," for winter-hardy varieties that are appropriate for outdoor structures.)

The term "climbing" rose is really a misnomer, because roses require assistance to ascend a structure (unlike true climbers, which come equipped with attaching tendrils). You must tie or fasten a climbing rose to a support as it grows. Keep in mind that climbing roses are unlikely to take off and smother the structure immediately. In the first season, the root system of the rose becomes firmly established. Usually, by the end of the second year, climbing roses begin to take off.

An inviting arbor is laden with red climbing rose blossoms to frame a walkway.

Whatever type of support you select, be sure it is consistent with the architectural style of your home or garden. The material from which the structure is built should reflect the exterior of the house as well. Brick, stone, wood, iron, even plastic can be used. The main prerequisites for a rose structure is that they be weather resistant and robust enough to support what can become a crushing weight of rose canes. For a natural look, you can also train climbers against trees or tall shrubs.

Trellises

Trellises positioned against the house give climbing and rambling roses the lift they need to spread their blooms upward like a fountain of color. Climbers that take to a trellis are the beautiful red-and-white-striped old garden rose 'Variegata di Bologna,' 'American Pillar,' and 'Don Juan,' which also produces fragrant, long-stem blooms for cutting.

Arbors

Arbors can be as rustic as an arch made from rough-hewn logs to a fanciful and elaborate latticework structure complete with facing seats. Regardless of the style, arbors provide an impressive entrance from the street or a romantic walkway from one part of your yard to another. 'Blaze' and the climbing form of 'Cécile Brünner' are two roses that excel on arbors.

Pergolas

Pergolas are structures composed of parallel columns. Some pergolas are very elaborate freestanding structures with an open gridwork ceiling that create a magical walkway of blooming roses on all sides. These large structures grace many formal gardens and require considerable ground space. When covered with a climbing rose, pergolas attached to a house create an awning of blooms. Recommended roses for pergolas are 'American Pillar,' 'Blaze,' and 'New Dawn.'

Encrusted with the white blooms of a climbing roses, a garden gate beckons.

An awning of pink bloom overhangs a wooden walkway.

56

Fences and Walls

Fences are probably the most popular setting for roses. Train climbers along a split rail or picket fence to brighten up the wood and curve the straight lines. Espalier them against the side of a stockade fence or the wall of a house.

Fences can be built from weather-worn timbers or primly painted pickets. Regardless of the style, a fence can be camouflaged by a single climbing rose like the multicolored climber 'Joseph's Coat' growing over and through it or enhanced by a bed of roses growing in front of it. 'Lawrence Johnston,' a golden yellow climber has one, long-lasting show of bloom and looks splendid on a rustic wooden fence. A breathtaking combination is red 'Dublin Bay' afire on a white fence. Fences also work well as backdrops for shrub and landscape roses.

Walls are wonderful stages for cascading climbing roses. If you have a wall on your property, roses like 'Don Juan' and 'Golden Showers' will enhance its beauty. Training a rose to a wall is easy. Pull the new shoots of the plant sideways and attach them to the wall so the growth habit of the rose moves horizontally as well as vertically. Use rose-covered walls as backdrops for taller shrub and landscape roses and for beds of roses and perennial mixes, as well.

Other Places for Climbers

The use of climbers in the landscape is almost unlimited. If you have a porch or deck, let roses tie your garden to your house. Use climbers to sprawl across a roof or overhang, spilling into your outdoor living space. You also can use them to cover eaves and to outline windows and doors, adding graceful color to the outside of the house and softening hard corners. Let climbing roses ramble up posts, cover old tree stumps, or spill over a garden gate. They even can offer a solution to eyesores, allowing you to attractively screen out unwanted views.

Grown over a pergola or arbor, climbing roses look as good from underneath as they do from a distance.

Roses and Other Flowers

Roses can be effectively combined with annuals and perennials to produce an extraordinary choreography of color and texture. The main goal in this alliance is to produce harmonizing and uniform masses of color in your yard. Planted in formal borders or paired in informal groupings, roses, annuals, and perennials prove to be good neighbors.

To plant a mixed border, first, make sure you select perennials that are hardy in your zone. Check the plant's care tag or catalog description to find this information. Select perennials and annuals that can exist in the same sun and soil conditions that roses require. Shade-loving plants, for example, are not good companions for sun-loving roses. Check heights, too. You'll want a mixture of low, medium, and tall flowers that stay in scale with the rose varieties you are growing. Finally, with a grand palette of colors to choose from, be creative in blending the tints and hues offered by the wide variety of plants available.

Roses with Annuals

Use low-growing annuals to provide color to the front of the border and around the base of your roses. For a blue-and-white garden, plant low-growing annual lobelia or ageratum in front of a white hedge of 'Iceberg' or a massed group of 'Pascali.' Or double up climbing rose 'Handel' with a 'Heavenly Blue' morning glory on an arbor to create a duet of rose and blue flowers. Lacy white sweet alyssum or soft gray dusty-miller planted in front of heavy-headed old garden roses paint the perfect Victorian portrait. The single pink petals of dianthus mirror the lovely single blooms of 'Betty Prior.' Other colorful annuals suited for coupling with roses are torenia, nierembergia, dwarf zinnia, snapdragon, verbena, and petunia.

If you like the wild and rangy look of informal country gardens, plant taller annuals such as the bold yellow tithonia as a backdrop to an equally bold yellow rose such as 'Oregold.' Larkspur, hollyhocks, and nicotiana all lend a country air and are tall and robust enough to stand shoulder to shoulder with roses of the same height. Annuals are also useful planted near roses that bloom only once a year. As the last flush of yearly blooming roses begins to fade, annuals are ready to take over the color show.

Roses with Perennials

Pair perennials and roses for a low-maintenance garden or border. Peonies and early spring-blooming roses will produce vivid and fragrant blooms simultaneously. Clumps of purple siberian iris are lovely planted next to the elegant yellow blooms of 'Graham Thomas.' Back-of-the-border perennials such as foxglove and delphinium create a romantic pastel portrait when they are combined with pink 'Louise Odier' and white 'Boule de Neige.' Other perennials that do well when mixed with roses are daylilies, shasta daisies, coreopsis, columbine, gladiolus, poppies, penstemon, and cranesbill geranium. For late-season perennial bloom, plant aster and monarda.

Combine annuals, perennials, and roses in the same garden for optimum color and plant choice. Single-color gardens are dramatic and can be achieved with combinations of all three plant types. For an all-red garden, intermix red varieties of verbena and penstemon backed by a prolific climber such as 'Blaze' or 'Dortmund.' A romantic pink border starts from the ground up with 'Pink Palace' dianthus and blends into the soft pink blooms of 'Souvenir de la Malmaison.'

Roses of all colors mix well with the silver foliage of artemisia, santolina, gypsophila, and lamb's-ears. To create a stark contrast, pair ornamental grasses such as Japanese sedge, fountain grass, or blue oat grass with roses.

Plant a flowering vine with a climbing rose to fill in an arbor or trellis. While the rose establishes itself, the vine will produce color. When the rose starts climbing, the vine and rose can intertwine to produce a duet of color. Clematis is an excellent perennial vine.

Perennials and roses are paired in a border. Stagger the heights of the plants to best highlight the various partners.

Formal gardens,
where flowers
are grown in
geometric beds,
are ideal for
hybrid tea roses.

An arching border of annuals, perennials, and roses takes center stage in the backyard opposite.

Roses teamed with annual flowers offer color all summer.

Annual vines that provide instant color are sweet pea, hyacinth bean, scarlet runner bean, and morning glory.

In addition to perennials and annuals, consider including bulbs, especially the tender ones, to fill in spots of color among the roses. Lilies, gladiolas, dahlias, canna lilies, freesia, and many others are perfect for instant companionship and for filling in unsightly bare spaces in the garden.

Roses and Trees and Shrubs

Annuals, perennials, and bulbs aren't the only companions for roses. Shrubs or a small ornamental tree makes a lovely companion. Use roses with shrubs to extend the blooming period of spring-flowering forsythia, spirea, azaleas, lilacs, viburnum, or beauty bush. Or use them to provide a colorful complement for summer-flowering shrubs such as weigela, mock orange, abelia, rose of sharon, or hydrangea.

In spring, blooms from cherry trees, magnolia, dogwood, flowering peach, crab apple, and hawthorn fill the air before the roses show their blooms. Later, the tree provides a pretty place to rest beneath. Place the tree so the roses are in its shade in the afternoon, and add a bench so you can sit and enjoy the garden. Don't plant roses too close to the tree, however, or they will fight for sun, food, and water.

Roses and Other Plants

If medicinal and culinary uses of roses interest you, try pairing roses with herbs or vegetables. Lavender planted as a border is a good complement for roses. Edge rose beds with sage, thyme, or parsley. Other herbs to mix with roses include globe basil, garlic chives, thyme, rosemary, and germander.

Vegetables love the same things roses do—sun, rich soil, food, and water. Plant roses in front of a trellis bearing vegetables such as

cucumbers, beans, or squash. Roses also can be planted between tomatoes and peppers. Where you're short on space, grow one of the underground crops, such as beets, carrots, and onions, between rose bushes.

When mixing roses with edible plants, be careful in the use of pesticides. Read labels to be sure the chemical is suitable for crops and to determine how long you must wait between spraying and harvesting. Some commonly sold pesticides are harmful to vegetable crops.

Companions for roses aren't limited to plants either. Statues, sundials, birdhouses, bird baths, garden lights, or small pools are just a few of the many types of accouterments that add interest to a rose garden.

Create an old-fashioned flower border
with roses and other classic perennials.

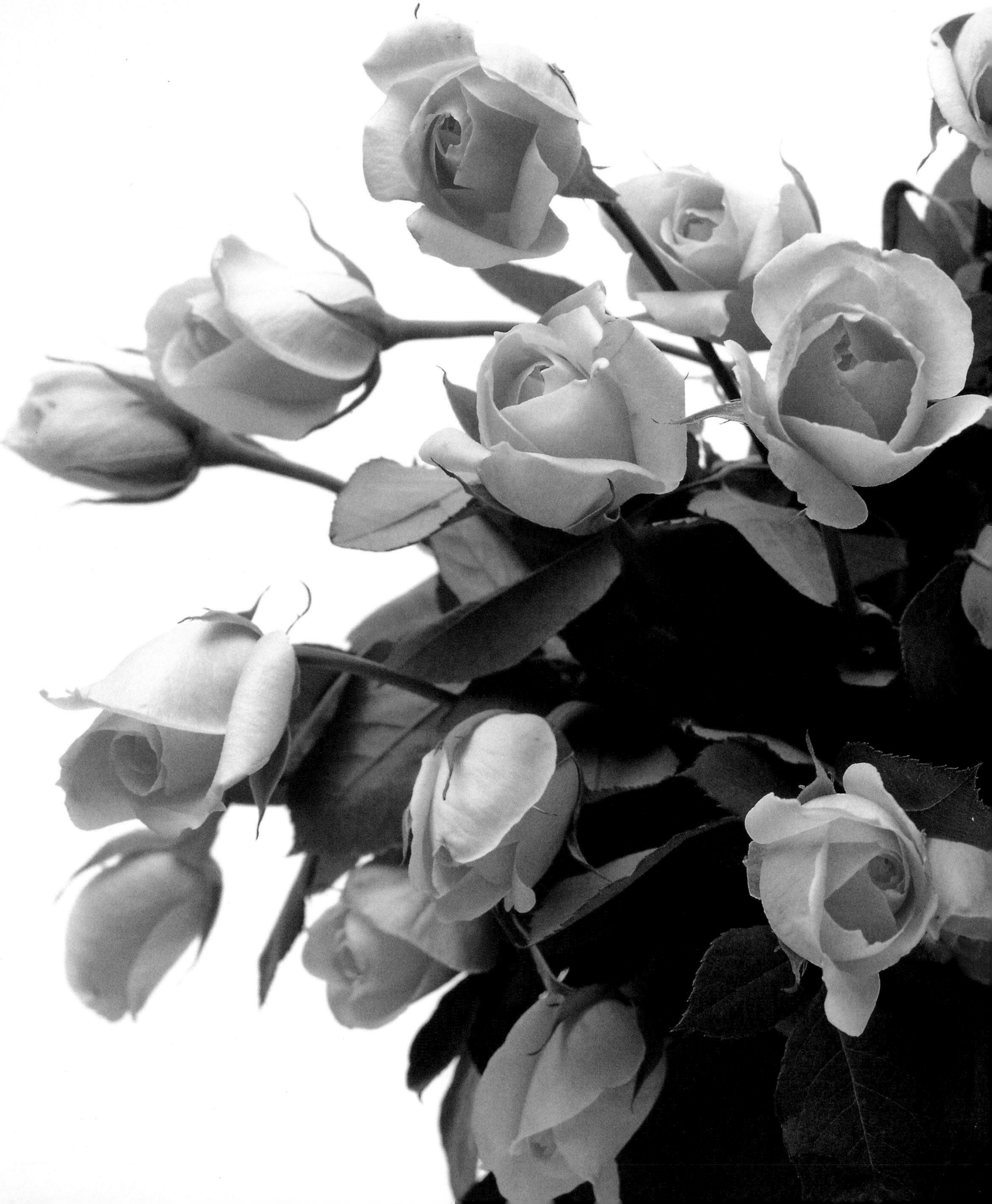

4

Portfolio
of Roses

Although roses can be classified into a great many categories, this book simplifies the selection process by breaking them into seven groups: hybrid teas, grandifloras, floribundas, climbers/ramblers, miniatures, old garden roses, and shrub and landscape roses. Most are available at garden centers, at nurseries, or through the mail.

Barbara Bush

HYBRID TEA

The hybrid tea represents the classic form of the rose: an elegant bud that unfolds into a high-centered bloom. In addition to its great beauty, the hybrid tea is a hardworking plant in the garden and landscape. This rose class offers a wide selection of color, size, and shape and is extremely versatile. The tall, elegant stature and extraordinary blooms of the hybrid tea are a standard in formal gardens but are equally at home as shrubs and in less formal settings. The free-flowering hybrid tea is splendid in massed display, planted singly among perennials in a border, as a hedge, or in containers. Loved for its beauty and fragrance, the hybrid tea often is planted in cutting gardens exclusively for its glorious yield.

American Pride

Color: Medium to dark red.

Flower Characteristics: Short, oval buds open to double, cupped blooms, 4 to 5 inches across with 45 to 50 petals. Flowers are lightly scented and bloom singly on long stems in early summer and fall.

Plant Characteristics: Medium tall. Winter hardy and disease resistant.

Barbara Bush

Color: Pink/white blend.

Flower Characteristics: Pointed buds open to lightly fragrant, 5-inch blooms with 30 to 35 petals. Continuous all-season bloom.

Plant Characteristics: Medium tall. Disease resistant. Related to 'Pristine.' Named to honor the First Lady.

Bewitched

Color: Medium pink with yellow stamens.

Flower Characteristics: Large buds open to 5-inch, double blooms with 24 to 30 petals. Flowers have a strong rose fragrance and are borne on long, strong, stiff stems. Profuse and continuous all-season bloom.

Plant Characteristics: Medium tall, upright, and very vigorous. An excellent cut flower because of its long vase life and extraordinary scent. All-America Rose Selections (AARS) winner.

Bing Crosby

Color: Red-orange.

Flower Characteristics: Classic buds open to flowers with 40 to 50 petals. Blooms are borne on long, straight stems.

Plant Characteristics: Medium tall. Named for the entertainer. All-America Rose Selections (AARS) winner.

Blue Girl

Color: Silvery lavender.

Flower Characteristics: Large blooms,

more than 5 inches across are borne on strong, long stems.

Plant Characteristics: Vigorous. One of the older lavender roses.

Brandy

Color: Apricot blend with bright golden stamens.

Flower Characteristics: Long, pointed buds open to 5- to 6-inch, double blooms with 25 to 30 petals. Flower form is informal and loose. Exhibits a tea fragrance. Blooms profusely all season.

Plant Characteristics: Medium tall, upright, and vigorous. Disease resistant except for black spot. Winter hardy with some protection. Good cut flower because of the classically formed blooms. All-America Rose Selections (AARS) winner.

Brigadoon

Color: Deep coral pink shades to lighter pink at base with creamy reverse; ever-changing color.

Flower Characteristics: Large, pointed buds open to 5-inch double blooms with 30 to 35 petals. This rose is a classic hybrid tea shape and flowers grow one per stem.

Abundant bloom all season.

Plant Characteristics: Medium tall. Very disease resistant. Excellent cutting flower because of its unusual color. Related to 'Pristine.' All-America Rose Selections (AARS) winner.

Cary Grant

Color: Orange blended with yellow.

Flower Characteristics: 5-inch flowers with 35 to 40 petals are borne on long, strong stems. The large blossoms are scented with a strong, spicy fragrance and are slow to open.

Brigadoon

Plant Characteristics: Medium tall, vigorous, upright, and bushy. Disease resistant and hardy. Named for the actor.

Charlotte Armstrong

Color: Deep pink.

Flower Characteristics: Long, slender buds open to fragrant pink blooms with long petals. The bloom is loose and informal and is borne on long stems. Profuse early bloom with moderate repeat.

Plant Characteristics: Medium tall, upright, vigorous, and compact. Disease resistant. A climbing form is available. An excellent cut flower. All-America Rose Selections (AARS) winner.

Chicago Peace

Color: Deep pink that grows into strong yellow at base with some streaks of pink, yellow, and apricot.

Flower Characteristics: Blooms are more than 5 inches wide, very double, and have 50 to 60 petals. Showy, fragrant blooms are even and full form. Good all-season bloom.

Plant Characteristics: Tall, spreading, upright, vigorous, and bushy. Disease resistant and winter hardy. Offspring of 'Peace'; exhibits similar characteristics except for its color.

Christian Dior

Color: Medium red.

Flower Characteristics: Very double blooms have 50 to 60 petals. The lightly scented, cup-shape blooms are borne on long stems. Midseason bloom with fair repeat.

Plant Characteristics: Medium tall. Petals burn in hot and dry settings, so plant them in spots with afternoon shade. This is an excellent cutting rose because of its fragrance, long stems, and long vase life. All-America Rose Selections (AARS) winner.

Chrysler Imperial

Color: Deep red.

Flower Characteristics: Long tapered buds open to 4- to 5-inch, double blooms with 40 to 50 petals. Open blooms are full, evenly petaled, and exhibit a true rose fragrance. Profuse midseason bloom with good repeat.

Plant Characteristics: Medium tall, erect, compact, and vigorous. Good in hot weather; prone to mildew. Good choice for small gardens. Originated from a cross between 'Charlotte Armstrong' and 'Mirandy.' A good cut flower. A climbing form is available. All-America Rose Selections (AARS) winner.

Color Magic

Color: Ivory to deep pink; color deepens when exposed to sunlight.

Flower Characteristics: Long buds open to double, 20- to 30-petaled blooms. Opens to a circular form that becomes cupped. Light fragrance. Continuous all-season bloom in both singles or clusters.

Plant Characteristics: Medium tall, upright, and well branched. Tender in cold climates and prone to fungal diseases. A good cut flower. All-America Rose Selections (AARS) winner.

Crimson Glory

Color: Red; takes on purplish tone in strong light.

Flower Characteristics: The double blooms, with about 30 petals, are borne on short stems. Excellent true rose fragrance. Good all-season show.

Plant Characteristics: Small and upright. Does not like full sun. Use in beds. A climbing form is available. This rose is noted for its color, fragrance, and petal texture.

Dainty Bess

Color: Pink.

Flower Characteristics: Long, slim buds open to five-petaled, fragrant blooms. The single petals frame maroon stamens and open flat to a 4-inch saucer-shape form. Good all-season bloom as a single or a cluster.

Plant Characteristics: Medium tall and

Double Delight

well branched. Exceptionally winter hardy. A climbing form is available. Long lasting both on the bush and in a bouquet.

Dolly Parton

Color: Scarlet.

Flower Characteristics: Large, pointed buds open to 6-inch double blooms with 30 to 35 petals. Good all-season bloom produces intensely fragrant flowers.

Plant Characteristics: Medium-tall plant produces blooms that are long lasting on the bush and as a cut flower. Progeny of 'Fragrant Cloud,' this rose is excellent for cutting because of its long, strong stems, spicy sweet fragrance, and long vase life. Does well in hot weather; protect in colder climates. Named for the singer-actress.

Double Delight

Color: White-yellow with red edge; the red edge deepens in sunlight.

Flower Characteristics: Long, pointed buds open to double, 5- to 6-inch blooms with 35 to 45 petals. Well-shaped blooms are scented with a spicy fragrance. Excellent all-season bloom; very free-flowering.

Plant Characteristics: Medium height, upright, spreading, and very bushy. Origins are 'Granada' and 'Garden Party.' Use for beds, in containers, or as cut flowers. A popular cutting flower for its color, form, fragrance, stem length, and long vase life. All-America Rose Selections (AARS) winner.

Dynasty

Color: Orange with yellow reverse.

Dynasty

Flower Characteristics: Long, pointed buds open to 4- to 5-inch blooms with 30 petals. Flowers are lightly fragrant and are borne on nearly thornless stems.

Plant Characteristics: Medium tall and upright.

Electron

Color: Deep pink to light crimson.

Flower Characteristics: Double, fragrant blooms with 32 petals; this rose has the classic form of the hybrid tea. Abundant all-season bloom.

Plant Characteristics: Grows to medium height and is upright, vigorous, and stocky. All-America Rose Selections (AARS) winner.

Fascination

Color: Orange/orange blend

Flower Characteristics: Double, cup-shape, classic hybrid tea blooms. Lightly fragrant. Not commonly seen, but a highly rated variety.

Plant Characteristics: Medium height. Vigorous, disease resistant, and winter hardy. A good choice for the middle of your rose border.

First Prize

Color: Rosy pink with lighter pink reverse.

Flower Characteristics: Huge, pointed buds open to 5- to 6-inch, double blooms with 20 to 35 petals. This rose has the classic form of the hybrid tea, is fragrant, and blooms singly on long stems. Good midseason bloom and good repeat.

Plant Characteristics: Medium height and vigorous. Needs protection in cold climates. A climbing type is available. A good cut flower because of its long vase life. All-America Rose Selections (AARS) winner.

Folklore

Color: Orange with yellow reverse.

Flower Characteristics: Large, pointed buds open to double, very fragrant blooms with 45 petals. Continuous seasonal bloom in clusters.

Plant Characteristics: Tall, vigorous, upright, and bushy. A relative of 'Fragrant Cloud.' Disease resistant and winter hardy. An excellent back of the border rose. Great form and strong fragrance make this a good rose for cutting. All-America Rose Selections (AARS) winner.

Forty-Niner

Color: Deep red with light yellow reverse.

Flower Characteristics: Flowers are lightly scented and bloom continuously all season.

Plant Characteristics: Strong growth with long branches. All-America Rose Selections (AARS) winner.

Fragrant Cloud

Color: Coral red turning purplish.

Flower Characteristics: Pointed buds open to 4- to 5-inch, double blooms with 25 to 30 petals. The large, evenly petaled blooms are intensely fragrant with a true rose scent. An early bloomer with good all-season bloom to follow.

Plant Characteristics: Medium height with long, spreading, free-branching stems.

Winter hardy and disease resistant. An excellent cutting rose because of its unforgettable fragrance, fine color, and long, elegant stems.

Garden Party

Color: Creamy white with light lavender pink edge.

Flower Characteristics: Large buds open to 5-inch, double blooms with 25 to 30 petals. Cup-shape flowers are lightly scented and have large, flaring petals. Profuse midseason bloom with good repeat.

Plant Characteristics: Tall, vigorous, strong, and bushy. Prone to mildew. Origins are 'Charlotte Armstrong' and 'Peace.' Plant 'Garden Party' in large groups or drifts for dramatic effect. May

develop black spot during wet wheather. All-America Rose Selections (AARS) winner.

Graceland

Color: Yellow.

Flower Characteristics: Short, pointed buds open to 4- to 5-inch blooms with 30 to 35 petals. Petal form is slightly ruffled. Blooms grow in long-stemmed clusters.

Plant Characteristics: Tall.

Granada

Color: Blend of pink, orange-red, and light yellow (a very colorful rose).

Flower Characteristics: Large, semidouble blooms nearly 5 inches across with 18 to 25 petals. Blooms as a single or

Fascination

in clusters and exhibits a spicy fragrance. Excellent all-season bloom.

Plant Characteristics: Tall, upright, vigorous, and bushy. Prone to mildew. Protect in colder climates. Good flower for cutting. All-America Rose Selections (AARS) winner.

Headliner

Color: White edged with red.

Flower Characteristics: Shapely buds open to very double blooms with slightly ruffled petals. Flowers exhibit a light fragrance. The red edge deepens in cooler weather. Abundant all-season bloom.

Plant Characteristics: Medium tall, upright, and vigorous. An excellent rose for cutting.

Helen Traubel

Color: Apricot flushed with pink.

Flower Characteristics: Double, nearly 5-inch blooms with 25 to 30 petals open to a cupped shape and exhibit a moderate

Headliner

fragrance. Good all-season bloom. Blooms as a single or in clusters.

Plant Characteristics: Medium height. Named for the opera singer. All-America Rose Selections (AARS) winner.

Honor

Color: Pure white.

Flower Characteristics: Long, pointed buds open to large, double blooms 4 to 5 inches with 20 to 22 petals. The lightly fragrant, loose blooms grow in singles or in clusters borne on long, strong stems. Good all-season bloom.

Plant Characteristics: Tall, upright, vigorous, and well branched. Prone to mildew in late summer and fall and is winter hardy. An excellent rose for cutting because of its long vase life. All-America Rose Selections (AARS) winner.

Ingrid Bergman

Color: Deep red.

Flower Characteristics: Fully double, velvety blooms. Very free-flowering.

Plant Characteristics: Medium height, upright, and vigorous. Disease resistant. Good edging or hedge rose. Named for the actress.

John F. Kennedy

Color: Pure white with green in center; as bloom matures, green shading disappears.

Flower Characteristics: Long buds open to 5- to 6-inch, double blooms with 45 to 50 petals. Fragrant, long-lasting blooms grow in singles or in clusters. Good all-season bloom.

Plant Characteristics: Medium height, upright, and moderately vigorous; compact. Disease resistant. Named for the 35th president of the United States.

Just Joey

Color: Orange/copper blend.

Flower Characteristics: Large, double blooms 4 to 6 inches across are very fragrant. Petals exhibit an unusual serrated edge with the coppery color paling to a lighter shade at its frilly edges. Abundant bloom in singles or in clusters.

Plant Characteristics: Medium height and spreading.

King's Ransom

Color: Pure deep yellow.

Flower Characteristics: Long, slender buds open to 5- to 6-inch, double blooms with 35 to 40 petals. The fragrant, cup-shape blooms grow in singles or in clusters and are borne on long, strong stems. Abundance of blooms early in the season with good repeat.

Plant Characteristics: Tall, upright, vigorous, and well branched. All-America Rose Selections (AARS) winner.

Legend

Lady X

Color: Pinkish lavender.

Flower Characteristics: Long buds open to double, lightly fragrant blooms with 35 to 40 petals. Blooms mostly as a single, but also as a cluster. Abundant all-season bloom.

Plant Characteristics: Tall, upright, well branched, and vigorous. Likes warm nights. This rose is a good choice for its color class. An excellent cut flower because of its fragrance and pretty pastel hue. Slightly arching canes are thorny and bear light green foliage.

Legend

Color: Bright red.

Flower Characteristics: Long buds open slowly to double, sweetly fragrant blooms with 30 petals borne on long stems. Abundant all-season bloom.

Plant Characteristics: Tall, disease resistant, and vigorous. Upright growth habit.

Lucille Ball

Color: Light apricot.

Flower Characteristics: Long, pointed buds open to 5-inch, double blooms with 30 petals. Moderately fragrant.

Plant Characteristics: Tall. Named for the comedienne.

Medallion

Color: Apricot yellow.

Flower Characteristics: Long, pointed buds open to very large, double blooms

Mikado

and compact. Disease resistant and winter hardy. Use in beds. Descended from 'Peace.' An excellent cutting rose because of its pastel hue and its long vase life.

Mikado

Color: Scarlet with gold at the base.

Flower Characteristics: Strongly fragrant with large, 4- to 5-inch blooms. Continuous seasonal bloom.

Plant Characteristics: Tall, well branched, upright, and slightly spreading. Disease resistant. All-America Rose Selections (AARS) winner.

Mirandy

Color: Dark red.

Flower Characteristics: Double, nearly 6-inch blooms with 40 to 50 petals exhibit a strong, true rose scent. Petals hold their dark red color instead of turning purplish. Good all-season bloom.

Plant Characteristics: Medium tall, upright, vigorous, and bushy. Very resistant to weather damage. All-America Rose Selections (AARS) winner.

Miss All-American Beauty

Color: Deep pink.

Flower Characteristics: Large buds open to very double, cup-shape blooms with 50 to 60 petals. The blooms exhibit an intense,

with 25 to 30 petals. Exhibits a fruity fragrance. Profuse midseason bloom with good repeat.

Plant Characteristics: Tall, upright, vigorous, and well branched. Thrives in hot weather and requires winter protection where temperatures drop below 20 degrees F. Relatively disease resistant. An excellent rose for cutting because of its long vase life. All-America Rose Selections (AARS) winner.

Michèle Meilland

Color: Pink with lilac shading, with hints of yellow and orange in the center.

Flower Characteristics: Slender buds open to large, double blooms with 35 to 40 petals. Lightly fragrant blooms borne on long, thin stems will bloom as a single or in clusters. Good staying power on the bush and in bouquets. Excellent all-season bloom.

Plant Characteristics: Small, upright,

true rose fragrance and grow in singles or in clusters. Abundant midseason bloom with good repeat.

Plant Characteristics: Tall, upright, vigorous, bushy, and spreading. Originally named for the opera singer, Maria Callas. All-America Rose Selections (AARS) winner.

Mister Lincoln

Color: Deep red.

Flower Characteristics: Double, fragrant, cup-shape blooms with 30 to 40 petals. Large flowers open to 4 to 6 inches across, have golden stamens, and are borne on long, elegant stems. Good all-season bloom, with good repeat.

Plant Characteristics: Tall, upright, vigorous, well branched, and healthiest of the dark reds. Descendant of 'Chrysler Imperial.' Most popular hybrid tea in the red color range. An excellent cutting rose because blooms are long lasting, are unfading in color, and exhibit the true rose scent. All-America Rose Selections (AARS) winner.

Mojave

Color: Apricot orange, tinted red.

Flower Characteristics: Large, double blooms nearly 4 inches across with 25 petals. Light, highly fragrant blooms grow in singles or in small terminal clusters.

Good all-season bloom.

Plant Characteristics: Medium height, upright, vigorous, and well branched. All-America Rose Selections (AARS) winner.

Oklahoma

Color: Maroon red.

Flower Characteristics: Long, pointed bud opens to very double bloom nearly 5 inches across with 40 to 55 petals. Very fragrant bloom retains its color without turning purplish. Abundant all-season bloom.

Plant Characteristics: Tall, upright, vigorous, and well branched. A climbing form is available.

Olympiad

Color: Medium red.

Flower Characteristics: Double blooms with 24 to 30 petals. Maintains its solid red color from start to finish. Bloom exhibits the classic hybrid tea form, with velvety petals and a light, fruity fragrance. Good all-season bloom in singles or in clusters.

Plant Characteristics: Medium tall, upright, vigorous, and compact. An excellent cutting rose because of its long stems, soft petals, and lasting vase life. All-America Rose Selections (AARS) winner in 1984. Olympiad was introduced as the official hybrid tea rose for the 1984 Olympic Games.

Oregold

Color: Deep golden yellow.

Flower Characteristics: Large, pointed buds, one to a stem, open to double, 5-inch blooms with 35 to 40 petals. Cup-shape blooms exhibit a light, fruity fragrance. Abundant midseason bloom with fair repeat.

Plant Characteristics: Medium tall, upright, well branched, and moderately vigorous. Prone to mildew. Protect in colder climates. Good cut flower because of its long vase life. All-America Rose Selections (AARS) winner.

Paradise

Color: Lavender blend; petals edged with red.

Flower Characteristics: Medium buds open to 5-inch, fragrant, semidouble blooms with 26 to 30 petals. Good all-season bloom.

Plant Characteristics: Medium height, upright, vigorous, and well branched. Mildew prone. Reasonably hardy. All-America Rose Selections (AARS) winner.

Pascali

Color: Pure white, flushed cream.

Flower Characteristics: Graceful buds open to 4-inch, double blooms with 25 to 30 petals. Classic hybrid tea blooms are lightly fragrant and are borne on long, strong stems. Excellent all-season bloom.

Plant Characteristics: Medium, vigorous, and bushy. Highly disease resistant and winter hardy. Considered the best of the white bedding roses because of its resistance to weather damage and disease. Most popular hybrid tea in the white color class. An excellent cutting flower. For best effect, plant a grouping of two or more. All-America Rose Selections (AARS) winner.

Peace

Color: Yellow, flushed with pink as it matures.

Flower Characteristics: Ovoid buds open to double, 5- to 6-inch blooms with 40 to 50 petals. The single blooms exhibit a light fragrance and are borne on strong stems. Good all-season bloom.

Plant Characteristics: Medium tall, upright, vigorous, and branching. Exhibits more vigor than the average bush. Very disease resistant. 'Peace' was hybridized in France in 1937 but was not sold until almost 10 years later. Budwood was smuggled out of France when Germany invaded during World War II. Given out at a United Nations meeting in San Francisco in 1945, 'Peace' marked the end of the war. The first rose to be named "World's Favorite Rose" and often referred to as "The Rose of the Century." Achieved the highest national rating in the United States. A climbing form is available. All-America Rose Selections (AARS) winner.

Peer Gynt

Color: Buttery, golden yellow that matures to peach at the edges.

Flower Characteristics: Very large, round, double blooms nearly 5 inches across. Abundant blooms are long lasting, have strong stems, and are very fragrant.

Plant Characteristics: Medium height; glossy green foliage.

Perfect Moment

Color: Yellow edged with red.

Flower Characteristics: Large buds open to lightly fragrant, classic hybrid tea blooms.

Plant Characteristics: Medium height, compact, bushy. Disease resistant. All-America Rose Selections (AARS) winner.

Perfect Moment

Peace

Flower Characteristics: Very double, nearly 6-inch blooms with 50 to 65 petals. Immensely fragrant blooms in the classic hybrid tea form. Good all-season bloom.

Plant Characteristics: Medium height, upright, vigorous, and bushy. Although 'Pink Peace' is related to 'Peace,' it does not resemble its namesake.

Precious Platinum

Color: Medium red.

Flower Characteristics: Double, medium-size blooms with 35 to 40 petals. The classic hybrid tea blooms have a light fragrance and grow as a single or in clusters. Abundant all-season bloom.

Plant Characteristics: Tall and upright. Disease resistant and winter hardy. Named by the platinum industry, which commissioned the rose.

Princesse de Monaco

Color: Ivory white edged with pink.

Flower Characteristics: Long buds open to double blooms with 30 to 40 large petals. The classic hybrid tea blooms are fragrant and they grow as singles. Blooms all season long

Plant Characteristics: Medium height, compact, upright, vigorous, and well branched. Relative of 'Peace.' Ideal as a bedding rose. An excellent cutting flower. Named for Princess Grace of Monaco.

Perfume Delight

Color: Deep pink.

Flower Characteristics: Long, large, pointed buds open to double, 5-inch blooms with 30 to 35 petals. Fragrance varies, but it is named for its strong perfume. Blooms are cup shaped and grow in singles or in a cluster. Abundant midseason bloom with fair repeat.

Plant Characteristics: Medium tall, upright, vigorous, and well branched with shiny green foilage. All-America Rose Selections (AARS) winner.

Pink Favorite

Color: Medium pink.

Flower Characteristics: Cup-shape double blooms measure 3 to 4 inches across and have 21 to 28 petals. The flowers are loose and lightly fragrant. Abundant all-season bloom.

Plant Characteristics: Medium, upright, vigorous, and bushy. Very thorny canes with glossy green foliage.

Pink Peace

Color: Medium to deep pink.

Pristine

Color: Ivory white edged with pale pink.

Flower Characteristics: Long, tapered buds open to 4- to 6-inch, double blooms with 25 to 35 petals. The single, fragrant blooms are camellia shaped and are borne on long stems. Good all-season bloom.

Plant Characteristics: Medium tall, upright, vigorous, and spreading. Excellent choice for bedding and cut flowers. Cut when buds are barely open for best show.

Rio Samba

Color: Yellow, turning scarlet as it opens.

Flower Characteristics: Pointed buds open to 5-inch blooms with 25 to 30 petals. The lightly fragrant, medium-size blooms grow one to a stem and sometimes in a cluster.

Plant Characteristics: Tall, vigorous, and slightly spreading. Disease resistant and hardy. Great color in the garden; best in cool weather. All-America Rose Selections (AARS) winner.

Royal Highness

Color: Light pink.

Flower Characteristics: Long buds open to more than 5-inch, double blooms with 35 to 50 petals. Classic hybrid tea blooms are fragrant and grow as a single or in a cluster on strong stems. Fair all-season bloom.

Sheer Bliss

Plant Characteristics: Tall, upright, and moderately vigorous. Prone to rust. Protect in colder climates. Excellent in beds and as cut flowers. All-America Rose Selections (AARS) winner.

Seashell

Color: Orange-red.

Flower Characteristics: Double blooms, 4 inches across with 35 to 50 overlapping petals. Classic hybrid tea blooms have a mild, fruity fragrance and grow as a single or in clusters on long stems. Free-flowering all season.

Plant Characteristics: Medium tall, upright, moderately vigorous, and well branched. All-America Rose Selections

(AARS) winner.

Sheer Bliss

Color: Creamy white flushed with pink.

Flower Characteristics: Long, large buds open to 4- to 5-inch blooms with 35 petals. Strong, perfumed blooms grow single to a stem.

Plant Characteristics: Medium tall, upright, and winter tolerant in most northern climates.

Sheer Elegance

Color: Pinkish coral blended with cream.

Flower Characteristics: Lightly fragrant, hybrid tea blooms are borne on strong stems.

Plant Characteristics: Medium height, upright, and robust. Disease resistant and winter hardy. All-America Rose Selections (AARS) winner.

Silver Jubilee

Color: Silvery pink blended with apricot.

Flower Characteristics: Double, long petaled blooms that are lightly fragrant. The blooms are abundant and are produced in clusters.

Plant Characteristics: Medium tall with dense foliage. Upright growth. The rose is disease free. It makes an excellent cutting flower. Commemorates H. M. Queen Elizabeth II's first 25 years on the throne of England.

Sterling Silver

Color: Silver lavender.

Flower Characteristics: Long, slender buds open to 3- to 4-inch double blooms with 30 petals. The blooms exhibit a light lemon scent and are the classic hybrid tea form. Blooms as a single or in a cluster. Fair all-season bloom.

Plant Characteristics: Medium tall, upright, and well branched. A good choice for the lavender or mauve color class because of its bloom and color. A climbing form is available. Canes are relatively thornless.

Summer Sunshine

Color: Bright yellow.

Flower Characteristics: Long, pointed buds open to double, 4-inch blooms with 25 petals. The lightly fragrant, cup-shape blooms grow as a single or in a cluster. Excellent all-season bloom.

Plant Characteristics: Medium, upright, vigorous, and well branched.

Sutter's Gold

Color: Light orange-yellow flushed pink with scarlet veining.

Flower Characteristics: Double, 3-inch blooms with 30 to 35 petals borne on long, nearly thornless stems. Blooms exhibit a fruity fragrance and the classic hybrid tea form. Good all-season bloom.

Plant Characteristics: Medium height.

Considered the sweetest-scented yellow rose. Named to commemorate the 100-year anniversary of the discovery of gold at Sutter's Mill, California. All-America Rose Selections (AARS) winner.

Sweet Surrender

Color: Medium pink.

Flower Characteristics: Pointed buds open to 4- to 5-inch, double blooms with 40 to 44 petals. Large blooms grow as a single on long, strong stems and open flat. Exhibits a true rose fragrance. Fair all-season bloom.

Plant Characteristics: Tall, upright, and compact. Winter hardy. An excellent cutting flower. Foliage is large and bright green. All-America Rose Selections (AARS) winner.

Rio Samba

Tiffany

Tiffany

Color: Pink with yellow base.

Flower Characteristics: Slender, pointed buds open to semidouble, 5-inch blooms with 25 to 30 petals. Classic hybrid tea form, deeply fragrant, and borne on strong stems. Good all-season bloom as a single or in clusters.

Plant Characteristics: Medium tall, upright, very vigorous, and bushy. A climbing form is available. An excellent rose for cutting. All-America Rose Selections (AARS) winner.

Touch of Class

Color: Pink shading to coral.

Flower Characteristics: Long, tapered buds open to large 4- to 5-inch blooms with 30 to 35 petals. The lightly fragrant blooms have a hint of a ruffle to the petals and are borne on long, strong stems.

Plant Characteristics: Tall and upright. Disease resistant and winter hardy. A good rose for cutting. All-America Rose Selections (AARS) winner.

Tropicana

Color: Orange-red.

Flower Characteristics: Large, pointed buds open to double 3- to 6-inch, cup-shape blooms with 30 to 35 petals. Lightly fruit-scented blooms grow as a single, or several in a cluster, on long stems. Excellent all-season bloom. Blooms hold their color even in the hottest sun.

Plant Characteristics: Medium, upright, vigorous, and well branched. Disease resistant, except to mildew. This was the first fluorescent orange rose. A climbing form is available. Excellent for cutting because of its fragrance, long stems, and long vase life. All-America Rose Selections (AARS) winner.

Unforgettable

Color: Pink.

Unforgettable

Flower Characteristics: Long, pointed buds open to slightly ruffled double blooms that measure more than 5 inches across and have 35 petals. Blooms are borne on long, straight stems. Lightly fragrant.

Plant Characteristics: Tall and vigorous. Excellent cutting rose because of its long stems and long vase life.

Voodoo

Color: Yellow peach blushing to scarlet.

Flower Characteristics: Blooms are the classic hybrid tea form with a fruity fragrance.

Plant Characteristics: Tall, upright, and vigorous. Disease resistant. All-America Rose Selections (AARS) winner.

Whiskey Mac

Color: Orange blended with yellow.

Flower Characteristics: Large, double blooms that are very fragrant. Fairly continuous bloom and very free-flowering.

Plant Characteristics: Small, vigorous, bushy, and low.

White Masterpiece

Color: Creamy white.

Flower Characteristics: Very double, large blooms with 50 to 60 petals. Classic hybrid tea form with a light fragrance. All-season bloom.

Plant Characteristics: Medium tall,

Yankee Doodle

upright, moderately vigorous, and compact.

Yankee Doodle

Color: Apricot with yellow and pink shading.

Flower Characteristics: Urn-shaped buds open to very double blooms that measure 4 inches across and have 75 petals. Flowers are lightly scented and bloom abundantly all season long.

Plant Characteristics: Medium tall, upright, very disease resistant, and winter hardy. All-America Rose Selections (AARS) winner.

GRANDIFLORA

For a great show of bloom and vigor, the grandiflora is an excellent choice. This rose class, not recognized in Europe, is a cross between hybrid teas and floribundas. The plants exhibit the best traits of their parents by producing large, vigorous bushes with continuous clusters of classic blooms. Grandifloras are tall and serve as excellent hedges, screens, and backdrops to other roses in a border. Planted singly, they make a dramatic show of color. Grandifloras are the rose of choice to mix with taller perennials; they are not a rose that gets lost in the crowd. Thanks to their hybrid tea parentage, grandifloras produce long-stem blooms that excel for cuttings and arrangements. Because of their continuous bloom, vigor, and foliage, grandifloras are an excellent choice for any type of rose garden.

Cherry-Vanilla

Color: Pink blend.

Flower Characteristics: Large, double blooms appear all summer long. The flowers are slightly fragrant with classic form. A relatively rare variety that's not generally available.

Plant Characteristics: Medium tall with upright canes. The plants are slightly thorny with average-sized, dark green foliage. Not reliably winter hardy in northern climates. Because of its height Cherry-Vanilla is a good choice for the back of the rose border. You can also use it as a single specimen plant.

Gold Medal

Color: Deep yellow tipped with orange-red.

Flower Characteristics: Large, long pointed buds open to 3- to 4-inch, double blooms with 35 to 40 petals. Blooms with a light, fruity fragrance in singles or in clusters. Good all-season show.

Plant Characteristics: Tall, upright, vigorous, and bushy. Disease resistant and hardy.

Love

Color: Red with white reverse.

Flower Characteristics: Two-tone buds open to double, cupped blooms with 24 to 30 petals. Classic hybrid tea blooms are lightly fragrant. Continuous bloom throughout the season.

Plant Characteristics: Medium height and upright. All-America Rose Selections (AARS) winner.

Pink Parfait

Color: Light to medium pink.

Flower Characteristics: Double 4-inch blooms with 20 to 25 petals. Cup-shape blooms are lightly fragrant and grow in singles or in clusters. Abundant midseason bloom with good repeat.

Plant Characteristics: Medium height, upright, vigorous, bushy, and hardy. All-America Rose Selections (AARS) winner.

Prima Donna

Color: Deep fuchsia pink.

Flower Characteristics: Profuse blooms borne on long, strong stems. Abundant all-season bloom.

Plant Characteristics: Tall, hardy, and disease resistant. Excellent rose for cutting because of its long stems and long-lasting

vase life. Also grows well in containers. All-America Rose Selections (AARS) winner.

Queen Elizabeth

Color: Pure soft pink.

Flower Characteristics: Pointed buds open to 3- to 4-inch, double blooms with 30 to 40 petals. Cup-shape blooms are loose and lightly tea scented, borne on long, nearly thornless stems. Abundant midseason bloom with excellent repeat. Blooms as a single or in clusters.

Plant Characteristics: Tall and vigorous. Disease resistant. Often considered the prototype of the perfect grandiflora. A climbing variety is available. Plant individually or in groups; can be used as a hedge. Excellent cut flower. Often considered to be the best pink rose ever developed. All-America Rose Selections (AARS) winner.

Shreveport

Color: Amber orange blend.

Flower Characteristics: Double, cup-shape blooms with 24 to 30 petals. Lightly fragrant. Fair all-season bloom.

Plant Characteristics: Tall. Hardy and relatively disease resistant. Excellent cutting rose because of its long stems and vase life. Named for the Louisiana city that is home to the American Rose Society. All-

Cherry-Vanilla

America Rose Selections (AARS) winner.

Solitude

Color: Coral orange with pink tinge and yellow reverse.

Flower Characteristics: Pointed buds open to 4- to 5-inch blooms with 32 to 35 petals. Blooms have a light, spicy scent and petals are scalloped along the edge. Opens quickly but holds bloom for a long time. The plants are in almost constant bloom from early summer until fall.

Plant Characteristics: Tall, upright, bushy, and hardy. All-America Rose Selections (AARS) winner.

Sonia

Color: Light pink.

Flower Characteristics: Classic tall buds open to 4-inch, semidouble blooms. Lightly fragrant blooms grow as singles or in clusters borne on long, graceful stems. Profuse and continuous bloom throughout the growing season.

Plant Characteristics: Small, upright, and loose. Popular florist rose. Blooms are long lasting.

Tournament of Roses

Tournament of Roses

Color: Two-tone pink.

Flower Characteristics: Very double blooms measure 4 inches across and grow in abundant clusters. Lightly scented.

Plant Characteristics: Medium tall, upright, and vigorous. Highly disease resistant and cold hardy. Excellent cut flower because it is both long lasting and fragrant. It was the official rose of the Tournament of Roses parade. All-America Rose Selections (AARS) winner.

FLORIBUNDA

Floribundas excel as landscaping and bedding roses. They require little care and attention and produce large patches of sustained color. Available in a wide array of colors, floribundas bear classic blooms in abundant clusters. Their low height, tidy form, and quick repeat bloom make them excellent choices for any garden. Planted in mass, floribundas provide a brilliant show of color and blooms. They are popular borders and work well in the landscape as hedges. Floribundas also can be planted in pots, planters, or tubs for concentrated bursts of bloom.

Accent

Color: Red

Flower Characteristics: Double, loose blooms are borne in clusters. Excellent continuous blooms all season.

Plant Characteristics: Compact growth makes it a good choice for containers. A seldom-seen introduction from the 1960s.

Amber Queen

Color: Amber yellow.

Flower Characteristics: Fragrant clusters of 5 to 7 blooms per stem. Produces attractive hollylike foliage.

Plant Characteristics: Medium tall and spreading. Disease resistant. All-America Rose Selections (AARS) winner.

Angel Face

Color: Lavender with ruby blush.

Flower Characteristics: Pointed buds open to cup-shape, double, 4-inch blooms with 35 to 40 petals. Blooms are extremely fragrant and produce ruffled petals and yellow stamens. Blooms as a single or in a cluster. Midseason bloom with good repeat.

Plant Characteristics: Medium height, upright, bushy, and compact. Disease resistant. A climbing form is available. All-America Rose Selections (AARS) winner.

Apricot Nectar

Color: Apricot pink fading to yellow center.

Flower Characteristics: Double, 4-inch blooms with 35 petals. Blooms are cup shaped, bear a fruity scent, and grow as a single or in a cluster. Abundant midseason bloom with good repeat.

Plant Characteristics: Tall, upright, vigorous, and slender with dark green

Accent

leaves. All-America Rose Selections (AARS) winner.

Betty Prior

Color: Medium to deep pink with lighter interior and white center.

Flower Characteristics: Single, 5-petaled flowers. Lightly scented blooms are cupped, opening to a saucer shape. Free-flowering, especially in autumn. In cooler weather blooms become redder.

Plant Characteristics: Tall, stiff, upright, vigorous, and bushy. Disease resistant. Use as hedges, in groups, or as singles. Excellent for mass plantings.

Cathedral

Color: Apricot blend.

Flower Characteristics: Double blooms measure 4 to 5 inches across with 18 to 24 petals. Produces flowers midseason with good repeat. Lightly fragrant blooms are produced in small clusters. Also called 'Coventry Cathedral.'

Plant Characteristics: Medium tall, growing to 4 feet. Bushy. Disease resistant,

Amber Queen

but susceptible to black spot. Winter hardy. All-America Rose Selections (AARS) winner.

Cherish

Color: Shell pink.

Flower Characteristics: Long, pointed buds open to very double blooms that bear a slight cinnamon scent and are extremely long lasting. Abundant bloom all season.

Plant Characteristics: Compact and symmetrical. Disease resistant and hardy in all but the coldest climates.

Chinatown

Color: Yellow edged with pink.

Flower Characteristics: Double blooms measure 4 inches across and open flat. Flowers grow in clusters and exhibit an excellent fragrance. Continuous and abundant bloom. Also called 'Ville de Chine.'

Plant Characteristics: Medium. Very vigorous and has shrublike growth.

Circus

Color: Yellow changing to coral, pink, and red in sunlight.

Flower Characteristics: Very double, rosette-shape blooms with 45 to 55 petals. Blooms have gold stamens and spicy scent. Midseason bloom with good repeat.

Plant Characteristics: Tall, bushy, and spreading. All-America Rose Selections (AARS) winner.

Class Act

Color: Pure white.

Flower Characteristics: Blooms have light fragrance and yellow stamens.

Apricot Nectar

Plant Characteristics: Tall.

Escapade

Color: Light pink to lavender with white center.

Flower Characteristics: Semidouble, 3-inch blooms with 12 petals and golden yellow stamens. Blooms are produced in large clusters and are lightly fragrant. Good midseason bloom with new crops of blossoms appearing every few weeks right up until hard frost.

Plant Characteristics: Medium tall, upright, and vigorous.

Europeana

Color: Dark blood red.

Flower Characteristics: Semidouble 3-inch blooms with 15 to 20 petals. Lightly scented, blooms are cup shaped and grow in large sprays of flowers. Abundant midseason bloom with good repeat.

Plant Characteristics: Medium height and spread; compact. Very disease resistant. Popular exhibition rose. All-America Rose Selections (AARS) winner.

Eutin

Color: Deep red.

Flower Characteristics: Double, cup-shape blooms with 30 petals. Lightly scented blooms grow in large clusters on long stems. Mid- to late-season bloom,

Cathedral

continuous until frost.

Plant Characteristics: Medium tall upright, bushy, and spreading. A good hedge plant that is also winter hardy.

Evening Star

Color: White with pale yellow shading near the base.

Flower Characteristics: Double blooms with 35 petals. Lightly fragrant blooms reminiscent of hybrid teas grow as a single or in clusters on long stems. Midseason

bloom with fair repeat.

Plant Characteristics: Medium height, upright, vigorous, and bushy. Sold as a hybrid tea in Europe.

Eyepaint

Color: Scarlet edged with pink and a white center.

Flower Characteristics: Single blooms with 5 to 7 petals and gold stamens. Midseason bloom with good repeat. Free-flowering in large clusters.

First Edition

Plant Characteristics: Tall and vigorous. Bushy and spreading. This rose is one of the group called 'hand-painted roses,' so named because of their unusual colors. It can be used as a shrub rose in beds or as a hedge.

Fashion

Color: Coral to salmon peach.

Flower Characteristics: Double blooms about 3 inches across with 21 to 24 petals. The flower, with a classic hybrid tea form, is lightly fragrant and blooms as a single or in clusters. Blooms midseason with good repeat.

Plant Characteristics: Medium tall, upright, vigorous, and bushy. Plant in groups of same variety for dramatic show. A highly acclaimed floribunda. All-

America Rose Selections (AARS) winner.

First Edition

Color: Coral-orange.

Flower Characteristics: Small, pointed buds open to double blooms with 30 petals. Lightly fragrant, the hybrid-tea–form bloom grows in singles or in clusters. Continuous abundant bloom.

Plant Characteristics: Medium tall, broadly upright, and vigorous. Highly disease resistant. All-America Rose Selections (AARS) winner.

First Kiss

Color: Light pink.

Flower Characteristics: Buds open to 3- to 4-inch, lightly fragrant blooms with 20 to 25 petals. Very free-flowering with good repeat throughout the season.

Plant Characteristics: Medium height. Related to 'Sun Flare.'

French Lace

Color: Ivory-white.

Flower Characteristics: Pointed buds open to 4- to 5-inch, double blooms with 30 to 35 petals. Lightly spice-scented blooms are the classic hybrid tea form. Blooms grow in clusters of 6 or more. Good midseason bloom with good repeat.

Plant Characteristics: Medium height, upright, vigorous, and well branched.

Disease resistant and hardy. Combines the best of the hybrid tea with the extravagant blooms of the floribunda. All-America Rose Selections (AARS) winner.

Goldilocks

Color: Deep yellow fading to pale yellow.

Flower Characteristics: Ruffled, 3-inch blooms with 45 petals. Blooms are cup shaped, grow in clusters, and have little or no fragrance. Abundant midseason bloom with good repeat.

Plant Characteristics: Medium tall, vigorous, bushy, and spreading.

Iceberg

Color: Pure white.

Flower Characteristics: Long, pointed buds open to 2- to 4-inch blooms with 30 petals. Fragrant blooms are saucer shaped with yellow center and grow in loose, medium-size sprays the entire length of the branch. Early to midseason bloom with good repeat. Outer petals develop a faint pink tinge in autumn.

Plant Characteristics: Tall, robust, free-branching, and very vigorous. Disease resistant and winter hardy. The whitest floribunda, 'Iceberg' is the top white rose on the market. Its also an excellant variety for containers. A recurrent climbing variety is available. Suitable for hedges and for group bedding. Excellent cut flowers.

Intrigue

Color: Red-purple.

Flower Characteristics: Round buds open to 3-inch double blooms with 20 to 30 petals. Old rose scented, ruffled blooms grow in singles or in clusters on long stems. Good midseason bloom with good repeat.

Plant Characteristics: Medium height, vigorous, and upright. Hardy. All-America Rose Selections (AARS) winner.

Ivory Fashion

Color: Ivory white, sometimes shaded with yellow.

Flower Characteristics: Large, semidouble blooms 4 inches across with 15 to 18 petals and yellow stamens. Blooms in fragrant clusters. Abundant midseason bloom with good repeat.

Plant Characteristics: Medium tall, strong, and upright. All-America Rose Selections (AARS) winner.

Little Darling

Color: Pink brushed with apricot.

Flower Characteristics: Classic small buds open to 2½-inch double blooms with 24 to 30 petals. Blooms are open cup shaped, exhibit a spicy fragrance, and grow in clusters. Abundant early to midseason bloom with good repeat.

Plant Characteristics: Tall, upright, vigorous, and sturdy. Disease resistant and

Iceberg

Plant Characteristics: Medium, vigorous, and upright. Disease resistant except for mildew and blackspot.

Orangeade

Color: Pure orange.

Flower Characteristics: Large, semi-double blooms with 7 to 9 petals. Open blooms grow in large clusters and are lightly scented. Abundant midseason bloom with good repeat.

Plant Characteristics: Low height.

Pinocchio

Color: Salmon pink fading to yellow at base.

Flower Characteristics: Double, cupped blooms measure 2 to 3 inches across and exhibit a sweet fragrance. Profuse bloom in large compact clusters all season. Also called 'Rosenmärchen.'

Plant Characteristics: Bushy growth.

Pleasure

Color: Coral pink flushed with salmon and a hint of yellow at the base.

Flower Characteristics: Large, ruffled, 4-inch blooms with 30 to 35 petals. Clusters range from 5 to 7 blooms. Lightly fragrant with abundant all-season bloom.

Plant Characteristics: Medium height and upright. Very disease resistant. Good cutting flower.

hardy. Huge clusters of blooms weigh down the branches. Good shrub rose or hedge.

Nearly Wild

Color: Rosy pink.

Flower Characteristics: Long, pointed buds open to 5-petaled, single fragrant blooms. The flowers are borne en mass on long, arching stems.

Plant Characteristics: Medium height and bushy growth. Spreads rapidly.

Excellent ground cover for slopes or banks or in front of taller shrubs. Can also be trained over a low fence or stone wall. Very hardy. Prefers full sun.

Orange Sensation

Color: Apricot-orange.

Flower Characteristics: Double blooms are nearly 3 inches across with bright yellow stamens. Lightly fragrant. Blooms are produced in clusters continuously throughout the season.

Purple Tiger

Color: Purple and white striped.

Flower Characteristics: Long, pointed buds open to 4-inch blooms with 25 to 30 petals. Blooms exhibit a true rose scent. Abundant bloom.

Plant Characteristics: Medium tall and compact. Related to 'Intrigue.'

Redgold

Color: Golden yellow edged with red.

Flower Characteristics: The red tips do not develop unless exposed to strong sunlight. Double, fruit-scented blooms with 25 to 30 petals. Abundant bloom. This classic hybrid tea form blooms in singles or in clusters.

Plant Characteristics: Low, compact, vigorous, and bushy. It is excellant to use as a hedge or in a bed as a border in front. All-America Rose Selections (AARS) winner.

Sea Pearl

Color: Light pink fading to apricot yellow.

Flower Characteristics: Long buds open to large, double blooms with 24 petals. Hybrid-tea–form blooms grow in singles or in clusters. Profuse early to midseason bloom with good repeat.

Plant Characteristics: Medium tall, vigorous, and bushy. The rose is disease resistant and hardy. It makes a good cutting flower.

Orange Sensation

Spartan

Color: Orange-red

Flower Characteristics: Double blooms measure more than 3 inches across and exhibit the classic hybrid tea form. Fragrant and clustered blooms are produced all season.

Plant Characteristics: Bushy and low.

Showbiz

Color: Medium red.

Flower Characteristics: Round buds open to double, 3-inch blooms with 28 to 30 petals. Lightly scented, ruffled blooms grow in clusters. All-season bloom.

Plant Characteristics: Medium height, upright, and vigorous. All-America Rose Selections (AARS) winner.

Summer Fashion

Color: Creamy yellow edged with pink.

Flower Characteristics: Short bud opens to 4- to 5-inch blooms with 35 to 40 petals. As the bloom matures, the yellow softens

Pleasure

to cream and the pink darkens to red.

Plant Characteristics: Medium height. Very showy planted in groups

Pinocchio

Summer Snow

Color: Snow white.

Flower Characteristics: Abundant large clusters of pointed buds open to semidouble blooms with 18 to 24 petals. Good all-season bloom.

Plant Characteristics: Medium low, vigorous, and bushy. A climbing type is available. Excellent for mass plantings and borders. Makes a good low hedge around an herb or annual flower border. Generally winter hardy.

Redgold

Sun Flare

Color: Light to medium yellow.

Flower Characteristics: Classic small, pointed buds open to 3-inch double blooms with 27 to 30 petals. Cup-shape blooms grow in singles or in clusters and exhibit a licoricelike scent. Good all-season bloom.

Plant Characteristics: Medium tall, upright, vigorous, and spreading. Very disease resistant and hardy. All-America Rose Selections (AARS) winner.

Sweet Inspiration

Color: Pure pink.

Flower Characteristics: Pointed buds open to semidouble, 3- to 4-inch blooms with 25 to 30 petals. Lightly scented. Flowers early, with good repeat. May grow taller than the average floribunda so plant toward the back of the border.

Plant Characteristics: Low to medium height. Hardy and disease resistant. Good for low mass or border planting. All-America Rose Selections (AARS) winner.

Vogue

Color: Coral.

Flower Characteristics: Large, 4-inch blooms with 25 petals. Lightly fragrant blooms grow as singles or in a cluster.

Good all-season bloom.

Plant Characteristics: Low to medium height, upright, vigorous, and compact. All-America Rose Selections (AARS) winner.

CLIMBERS/RAMBLERS

Climbers and their relatives, the ramblers, are as versatile as they are beautiful. Trained to a trellis, pillar, arbor, fence, or wall, climbers will quickly smother their support with bloom. Climbers have mixed parentage, so height, color, and form will vary. These graceful roses generally need to be tied up to prevent toppling. Ramblers have long pliable canes with large clusters of small blooms. If left to their own devices, ramblers will spread freely in all directions.

Albertine

Color: Pink-copper.

Flower Characteristics: Red-tinted buds open to small, very fragrant blooms. Provides about 3 weeks of continuous bloom, but is not recurrent.

Plant Characteristics: A very well-

Spartan

Climbers at Old Westbury Gardens

known rambler, this rose can stand unsupported and does equally well trained to a pergola or arbor. Very fast growing and can reach lengths of 20 feet. Disease resistant except mildew prone.

Aloha

Color: Pink.

Flower Characteristics: Short buds open to 3- to 5-inch double blooms with 55 to 60 petals. Fragrant blooms are cup shaped with yellow stamens. Profuse bloom in midseason, and then again in the fall with good bloom in between.

Plant Characteristics: Upright, short growing, disease resistant, and winter hardy in northern gardens. There is no bush form of this climbing hybrid tea. A good choice for a pillar rose, it will reach 6 to 10 feet tall if you tie it as it grows. Also does well on a small or medium trellis or as a free-standing hedge. An excellent cutting flower because of its fragrance and strong, long stems.

Altissimo

Color: Blood red.

Flower Characteristics: Large, 5-inch, single, 7-petaled blooms open to reveal bright golden stamens. Early season bloom continues until late season with consistent and repeat flowering. Blooms have little scent, but their color is rich and nonfading.

Plant Characteristics: A climbing floribunda with restrained, upright growth. Long lasting and very weather resistant. Good for pillars or on a wall where it will reach 7 feet.

America

Color: Coral pink.

Flower Characteristics: Large, pointed buds open to 3- to 4-inch double blooms with 40 to 45 petals. Good midseason bloom with fair repeat. Blooms are spice scented and cup shaped.

Plant Characteristics: Upright, disease resistant, and winter hardy. Slow to climb. All-America Rose Selections (AARS) winner.

American Beauty

Color: Red.

Flower Characteristics: Large, cup-shape flowers are borne on long stems. Abundant spring bloom with intermittent repeat.

Plant Characteristics: Upright and vigorous. A good pillar rose as well as a climber. Blooms are good for cutting.

American Pillar

Color: Deep pink with white eye.

Flower Characteristics: Clustered blooms are 2 to 3 inches, single, and have 5 petals and yellow stamens. Very abundant early season bloom that lasts for several

months, but not recurrent. Blooms in tight clusters. Light fragrance.

Plant Characteristics: Rambler with 10- to 20-foot shoots. Upright, disease resistant except for mildew, and winter hardy. A good rose for pergolas and trellises.

Blaze

Color: Medium red.

Flower Characteristics: Clustered, cupped blossoms are 2 to 3 inches, are semidouble, and have 18 to 24 petals. Good midseason bloom lasts through the season. Improved form produces clusters of blooms on new and old canes. Lightly fragrant blooms hold their color even in the hottest sun.

Plant Characteristics: Upright, disease-resistant, and winter-hardy climber with 6- to 12-foot canes. This abundant bloomer is a good choice for pergolas, pillars, and arches or for planting along fences and porches.

Blossomtime

Color: Medium pink with deep pink reverse.

Flower Characteristics: Long, pointed buds open to highly fragrant, very double blooms that measure 3 to 4 inches across with 35 to 40 petals. Blooms in clusters. Good midseason bloom with sparse repeat.

Plant Characteristics: Upright, disease

resistant, and winter hardy in northern climates. A good rose for wooden trellises.

Butterscotch

Color: Yellow with orange reverse.

Flower Characteristics: Long buds open to double, cupped blooms that measure 4 to 5 inches across. Lightly fragrant blooms are produced in clusters all season long. Also called 'Jactan.'

Plant Characteristics: Grows 6 to 10 feet tall. A large-rose climber.

Cécile Brünner

Color: Light pink.

Flower Characteristics: Dainty buds open to small, 1½-inch double, sweetly scented blooms. Abundant early to midseason bloom that lasts for several weeks, then sporadic recurrent bloom until frost.

Plant Characteristics: Extremely

Butterscotch

vigorous climber with canes that extend 20 feet long. This rose is a climbing sport of the bush and is considered superior. Nearly a climbing miniature. Good for trellises, arbors, and walls. A fine cutting rose.

Dainty Bess

Color: Pink.

Flower Characteristics: Long, slender buds open to 4-inch single blooms with 5 petals and brownish stamens. This climber produces more bloom than the bush. Continuous bloom with good repeat.

Plant Characteristics: This climbing hybrid tea is a good choice for pillars.

Don Juan

Color: Deep red.

Flower Characteristics: Large buds open to classic, double, hybrid tea blooms 4 to 5 inches wide with 35 petals. The small singles or clusters of bloom are highly fragrant. Abundant bloom with fair repeat.

Plant Characteristics: Upright, disease resistant, but not always winter hardy. Makes an excellent pillar, wall, or trellis rose. A good cutting rose because of its long stems and heavy scent. Relative of 'New Dawn.'

Dorthy Perkins

Color: Medium pink.

Flower Characteristics: Double blooms

measure ¾ inch across, have 35 to 40 petals, and are borne on long stems. This plant produces great clusters of blooms only once, in late summer. Once a very popular rambler. Very fragrant.

Plant Characteristics: Grows 10 to 13 feet. Vigorous and winter hardy, but prone to mildew.

Dortmund

Color: Crimson red with white center.

Flower Characteristics: Large, fragrant clusters of single, 3- to 4-inch, 5-petaled blooms. Abundant midseason bloom with good repeat. Blooms open flat to show yellow stamens. Continuous bloom is improved by removing the flowers as they begin to fade.

Plant Characteristics: Medium tall, upright, disease resistant, and winter hardy. Suitable for all light conditions, but thrives on shady walls where it grows to 10 feet. This rose is a good choice for pillars and reaches 7 to 8 feet. Also can be used as a freestanding hedge.

Dublin Bay

Color: Medium red.

Flower Characteristics: Cupped, double blooms are fragrant, are 4 inches wide, and have 25 petals. Abundant midseason bloom with good repeat. Has a tendency to bloom from the ground up.

Fortune's Double Yellow

Plant Characteristics: Climbing floribunda that is upright, disease resistant, well branched, and winter hardy. Among the best of the shorter red climbers, but grows slowly. Behaves more like a shrub during the first several years. Looks best when grown on a low fence, stone wall, or wooden trellis. Relative of 'Altissimo.'

First Prize

Color: Ivory with pink flushed edges.

Flower Characteristics: Classic hybrid-tea–form blooms are borne on stems up to 18 inches long. Abundant blooms all summer.

Plant Characteristics: Vigorous and winter hardy. The climbing variety of 'First Prize' has canes that reach 8 to 10 feet. An excellent cutting flower because of its long stems and lovely flowers.

Fortune's Double Yellow

Color: Amber-yellow.

Flower Characteristics: Semidouble, loose, and extremely fragrant blooms are produced both as singles and in clusters. Blooms only once. Also called 'Beauty of Glazenwood.'

Plant Characteristics: Grows best in temperate climates and is not always winter hardy. Requires the support of a trellis or arbor. Grows to 8 feet.

Dorthy Perkins

Golden Showers

Color: Medium yellow.

Flower Characteristics: Small clusters of scented, semidouble blooms 4 to 5 inches wide with 25 to 35 petals. Cup-shape blooms are loose. Abundant bloom all season.

Plant Characteristics: Floribunda climber that is upright, disease resistant, bushy, and winter hardy except in extremely harsh winters.

Slow to start, but abundant thereafter; grown against a pillar, it may take several years to reach 6 feet. Although upright, it can be trained to fill lateral space and grows up to 10 feet on a wall. Most popular of all yellow climbers. Relative of 'Charlotte Armstrong.' All-America Rose Selections (AARS) winner.

Handel

Color: Creamy white with deep pink flushed edges.

Flower Characteristics: Shapely buds open to 3-inch, loosely double blooms with 20 petals. Abundant and profuse midseason blooms with good repeat flowering into autumn. Lightly scented.

Plant Characteristics: Tall. Floribunda climber that is very reliable, although prone to blackspot. A popular climber because of its unusually colored blooms.

Hi Ho

Color: Light red and deep pink.

Flower Characteristics: Small, double blooms. Profuse all-season bloom.

Plant Characteristics: A vigorous rose with medium growth. A climbing miniature that reaches 3 feet in height.

Joseph's Coat

Color: Bright yellow, maturing to orange, then red.

Flower Characteristics: Clustered, cupped, double blooms are 3 to 4 inches wide with 24 to 30 petals. Good midseason bloom with fair repeat. Lightly fragrant. A very colorful and ever-changing rose, with reds deepest in autumn.

Plant Characteristics: Upright, disease resistant, although not always winter hardy. A tall floribunda that can be trained like a climber, this rose will reach 10 feet. Train against a wall or fence in mild climates, otherwise the rose can be used as a shrub.

Lace Cascade

Color: White.

Flower Characteristics: Creamy buds open to pure white 4-inch blossoms.

Plant Characteristics: This vigorous rose can be grown as a shrub or trained to a fence, arbor or trellis. Grows to about 7 feet tall.

Lady Banks' Rose

Color: White

Flower Characteristics: Small, lightly fragrant double blooms. Abundant bloom in spring, but is not recurrent.

Plant Characteristics: Grows 20 feet in height. Requires full sun and flourishes in a warmer climate. Used as a hedge in some places. Also known as 'Rosa banksiae banksiae.'

Lawrence Johnston

Color: Golden yellow.

Flower Characteristics: Clusters of cupped, fragrant, semidouble blossoms 3 to 4 inches wide with 18 to 24 petals. A profuse and long-lasting bloom early in season, but not recurrent.

Plant Characteristics: Upright and very vigorous climber with growth up to 20 feet tall. Because the plant is so spreading it requires a large amount of space. Prone to blackspot, but winter hardy. Use to cover broad areas of sheltered walls or fences, or on a trellis.

Magnifica

Color: Red.

Hi Ho

Magnifica

Flower Characteristics: Semidouble, very fragrant blooms open to expose striking yellow stamens. Blooms only once, but very profusely.

Plant Characteristics: Grows 6 to 10 feet tall and makes an excellent hedge. Officially considered a shrub rose, but the long arching canes are suitable for being trained to an arbor, fence, wall, or trellis.

New Dawn

Color: Pale pink.

Flower Characteristics: Cupped blooms are semidouble, 3 to 4 inches wide with 18 to 24 petals. Fragrant blooms have bright yellow stamens. Good midseason bloom with flowers produced singly or in clusters throughout the summer.

Plant Characteristics: Upright, medium height, bushy, and disease resistant, Winter hardy. Slow growing but will reach 12 feet in height. Good for pillars or freestanding hedges.

Peace

Color: Yellow tinged with pink at edges.

Flower Characteristics: Classic hybrid-tea–form blooms are as lovely as the original 'Peace.' Good all-season bloom.

Plant Characteristics: Blooms on second-year growth only. Vigorous and grows 15 to 20 feet tall. Climbing sport of the popular 'Peace.'

Piñata

Color: Yellow with orange and red.

Flower Characteristics: Large, double blooms have 30 petals. Blooms in clusters all season with consistent repeat.

Plant Characteristics: This vigorous rose can stand alone as a shrub. Good climber for small gardens because of its compact size, 6 to 8 feet tall.

Royal Sunset

Color: Apricot.

Flower Characteristics: Classic hybrid tea, double 5-inch blooms have 20 petals and exhibit a fruity fragrance. Profuse bloom with good repeat. Color fades to peach as the weather warms.

Plant Characteristics: Not always winter hardy. In northern gardens the plants require added winter protection. Climbing hybrid tea is upright in habit and therefore good for pillars and walls.

Schoolgirl

Color: Orange-yellow.

Flower Characteristics: Shapely buds open to double, classic hybrid-tea–shape blooms. Good first bloom with fair repeat. A large-flowering climbing rose.

Plant Characteristics: Grows 8 to 10 feet tall. A good choice for training to a wall, or a fence. Vigorous climber, but prone to blackspot.

Show Garden

Color: Deep pink.

Flower Characteristics: Double blooms measure 4 to 5 inches across. Profuse all-season bloom.

Plant Characteristics: Vigorous, disease resistant, and winter hardy. Grows 6 to 7 feet in height.

Tiffany

Color: Medium pink and yellow blend.

Flower Characteristics: Long, pointed pink buds open to classic hybrid-tea–shape blooms 4 to 5 inches wide with 25 to 30 petals. Blooms abundantly all season long as a single or in clusters. Extremely fragrant.

Plant Characteristics: Vigorous and disease resistant. This rose is winter hardy in northern climates. Foliage is dark green and attractive. This popular hybrid tea is medium tall. All-America Rose Selections (AARS) winner.

White Cherokee

Color: Pure white.

Flower Characteristics: Single, fragrant, 5-petaled blooms in abundant clusters. Delicate yellow stamens. Early spring bloomer.

Plant Characteristics: Very aggressive climber, but not winter hardy in colder climates. State flower of Georgia.

Tiffany

White Dawn

Color: Pure white.

Flower Characteristics: Double, fragrant blooms have 35 petals and grow in clusters. Sweet rose fragrance. Long-lasting Camellialike blooms. Good all-season bloom with good repeat.

Plant Characteristics: Vigorous, winter hardy, disease resistant, and quickly spreads over a large area. Excellent border rose in gardens because the plants arch and trail.

MINIATURES

For beds, borders, containers, or hanging baskets, miniature roses are an excellent choice. These compact beauties rarely grow more than 18 inches tall, yet they bloom as abundantly as their taller cousins. Miniature roses are readily available in a wide assortment of colors, flower forms, and growth habits. Miniatures also are relatively winter hardy in northern gardens. Indoors, use miniature roses to brighten a winter windowsill.

Baby Katie

Color: Pink and cream blend.

Flower Characteristics: Double blooms. Produces abundant blooms all season.

Plant Characteristics: Compact plants are vigorous, disease resistant, and winter hardy in northern climates. A good choice

Climbing roses in an Oregon flower garden.

for containers.

Baby Betsy McCall

Color: Light pink.

Flower Characteristics: Dainty buds open to double, cupped blooms that measure 1 to 1½ inches across with 20 to 24 petals. The tiny flowers are very fragrant. Produces blooms midseason with good repeat.

Plant Characteristics: Upright, bushy, disease resistant, and winter hardy. Grows 12 to 18 inches tall and excels in edgings, borders, beds, and containers. Grows well indoors.

Beauty Secret

Color: Medium red.

Flower Characteristics: Long pointed buds open to double, classic hybrid-tea–form blooms 1½ inches across with 24 to 30 petals. The large blooms have a strong fragrance. Abundant midseason bloom with good repeat.

Plant Characteristics: Upright, disease resistant, well branched, and winter hardy. Grows 10 to 18 inches tall. The foliage is bright green and shiny.

Center Gold

Color: Deep yellow.

Flower Characteristics: Double, classic

Miniature rose border

hybrid-tea–form blooms measure 1½ inches across and have 25 to 35 petals. Fragrant and abundant flowers. Midseason bloom with good repeat.

Plant Characteristics: Upright, disease resistant, well branched, and winter hardy. Grows 14 to 18 inches tall. Good bedding rose has fine, long-lasting cut flowers. Also grows very well in window boxes, pots, or large planters.

Child's Play

Color: White edged with pink.

Flower Characteristics: Double, 2-inch blooms flower one to a stem. Abundant all-season bloom.

Plant Characteristics: Low, compact, well branched, and very disease resistant. Grows 15 to 20 inches tall. All-American Rose Selections (AARS) winner.

Cinderella

Color: Light pink.

Flower Characteristics: Very double, cupped blooms are only ¾ inch across and have 45 petals. Spicy fragrance. Profuse midseason bloom continues all season long.

Plant Characteristics: Upright, disease resistant, and winter hardy. This compact rose grows 8 to 10 inches tall and excels in beds, in rock gardens, and indoors through the winter. Very popular because of its micro-mini size and delicate, petite blooms.

Child's Play

A climbing variety also is available.

Cuddles

Color: Coral pink.

Flower Characteristics: Very double, classic hybrid-tea–form blooms are 1¼ inches across and have 55 to 60 petals. Blooms exhibit a light fragrance and are extremely long lasting. Profuse midseason bloom with good repeat.

Plant Characteristics: Vigorous, disease resistant, and winter hardy. Bushy rose; grows 14 to 16 inches tall. A good choice for beds, borders, containers, and indoors through the winter.

Cupcake

Color: Medium pink.

Flower Characteristics: Very double, classic hybrid-tea–form blooms are 1½ inches across and have 50 petals. Blooms exhibit little or light fragrance and are extremely long lasting. Blooms midseason with good repeat.

Plant Characteristics: Vigorous, disease resistant, and winter hardy. Bushy and compact; grows 12 to 14 inches tall.

Debut

Color: Red fading to white at base.

Flower Characteristics: Blooms measure 2 inches across and are extremely long lasting. Blooms are continuous and abundant .

Plant Characteristics: Grows 14 to 18 inches tall and spreads the width of its height. Mounded form. All-America Rose Selections (AARS) winner.

Dreamglo

Color: Red with white at base.

Flower Characteristics: Very double, classic hybrid-tea–form blooms are 1 inch across and have 50 petals. Blooms exhibit a light fragrance and are one to a stem. Abundant midseason bloom with good repeat.

Plant Characteristics: Upright, disease resistant, and winter hardy. Grows 18 to 24 inches tall and is excellent for beds and borders.

Galaxy

Color: Dark red.

Flower Characteristics: Double, cupped blooms are 1½ inches across and have 25 petals with light or little fragrance.

Abundant midseason bloom with good repeat.

Plant Characteristics: Upright and bushy. Disease resistant and winter hardy. This compact rose grows 12 inches tall and does well in beds, in borders, and as an edging. Grows well in hot weather and indoors.

Gold Coin

Color: Deep yellow.

Flower Characteristics: Double, cupped to flat blooms are 1½ inches across and have 24 to 30 petals with strong fragrance. Excellent midseason bloom with good repeat.

Plant Characteristics: Compact, disease resistant, and winter hardy. This low, tidy rose grows 8 to 12 inches tall. A very popular rose because of its small stature and because of its fragrant, diminutive blooms.

Golden Halo

Color: Yellow.

Flower Characteristics: Double, classic hybrid-tea–form blooms are fragrant and profuse. This rose produces abundant all-season bloom.

Plant Characteristics: Bushy, disease resistant, and winter hardy. Grows 16 to 20 inches tall. A good choice for beds, borders or containers.

Good Morning America

Color: Yellow.

Flower Characteristics: Double, classic hybrid-tea–form blooms are fragrant and one to a stem. Petals are tipped with red in bright sunlight.

Plant Characteristics: Upright, disease resistant, and winter hardy. Grows 16 to 24 inches tall and is a fine cutting flower.

Green Ice

Color: Whitish pink that gradually matures to a light green.

Flower Characteristics: Double, classic hybrid-tea–form blooms are 1¼ inches across and have 30 petals with light fragrance. Grows in heavy clusters. Excellent midseason bloom.

Plant Characteristics: Disease resistant and winter hardy. This dwarf rose grows 8 inches tall and spreads out to 16 inches, which makes it a good choice for hanging baskets. Its long pliable canes also allow it to be trained to a trellis.

Holy Toledo

Color: Orange fading to yellow at base.

Flower Characteristics: Double, classic hybrid-tea–form blooms are 1¾ inches across and have 25 petals. Blooms exhibit a light fragrance. Blooms midseason with good repeat.

Plant Characteristics: Disease resistant, but not always winter hardy. This bushy rose grows 15 to 18 inches tall and is a fine choice for beds and borders.

Hula Girl

Color: Orange-salmon.

Flower Characteristics: Long, pointed buds open to double blooms with 25 to 40 petals. Fruity scent. Abundant midseason bloom with good repeat.

Plant Characteristics: Grows to 12 inches tall and is very bushy. Disease resistant and winter hardy. Excellent choice for beds, borders, and edgings. Also excels in containers.

Ice Queen

Color: White.

Flower Characteristics: Very double blooms are long lasting.

Plant Characteristics: Disease resistant and winter hardy. Grows 12 to 14 inches tall and is a good choice for beds, borders, window boxes, and hanging baskets. In cool weather this rose has a tendency to develop a slightly pink tinge. A white sport of 'Cupcake.'

Jean Kenneally

Color: Apricot.

Flower Characteristics: Double, classic hybrid-tea–form blooms are 1½ inches

Debut

across and have 24 to 30 petals. Blossoms exhibit a light fragrance. Midseason bloom with excellent repeat.

Plant Characteristics: Upright, well branched, disease resistant, and winter hardy. Bushy; grows 22 to 30 inches tall Use in beds, borders, and edgings. Grows well indoors on a sunny windowsill.

Julie Ann

Color: Orange-red.

Flower Characteristics: Double, classic hybrid-tea–form blooms are 1½ inches across and have 24 to 30 petals. Blossoms exhibit a strong fragrance. Midseason bloom with good repeat.

Plant Characteristics: Upright, disease resistant, and winter hardy. This bushy rose grows 10 to 14 inches tall and is an excellent choice for beds or containers. Grows well indoors.

Kathy

Color: Medium red.

Flower Characteristics: Double, classic hybrid-tea–form blooms are 1½ inches across and have 24 to 30 petals. Blossoms exhibit a strong fragrance. Midseason bloom with continuous repeat.

Plant Characteristics: Disease resistant and winter hardy. This compact rose grows 8 to 10 inches tall. Its tendency toward spreading makes it a good choice for

hanging baskets, window boxes, or containers. Grows well indoors.

Kristin

Color: White, deeply edged with red.

Flower Characteristics: Urn-shape buds open to classic hybrid-tea–form blooms. One bloom per stem.

Plant Characteristics: Disease resistant and winter hardy. Grows 20 to 24 inches in height. Makes an attractive edging plant in

rose or perennial borders.

Lavender Jewel

Color: Mauve.

Flower Characteristics: Semidouble, cupped blooms are 1½ inches across and have 12 to 20 petals. Large blossoms exhibit a light fragrance. Blooms in singles or in clusters. Midseason bloom with good repeat.

Plant Characteristics: Disease resistant

Hula Girl

Ice Queen

and winter hardy. This rose grows 10 inches tall and spreads out 15 inches. Its long pliable canes make it an excellent choice for hanging baskets or window boxes.

Magic Carrousel

Color: White edged with red.

Flower Characteristics: Semidouble, cupped to flat blooms measure 1¾ to 2 inches across and have 12 to 20 petals. The blooms exhibit a light fragrance. Midseason bloom with good repeat.

Plant Characteristics: Extremely vigorous, spreading, disease resistant, and winter hardy. Grows 15 to 18 inches tall, sometimes reaching 30 inches. A fine rose for beds and borders. Pinch back to avoid legginess.

Minnie Pearl

Color: Coral pink flushed with salmon.

Flower Characteristics: Long, delicate

buds open to double blooms, one to a stem. Abundant blooms.

Plant Characteristics: Vigorous and disease resistant. Grows 18 to 24 inches tall on a rounded, well-shaped bush. Use for beds or borders.

My Sunshine

Color: Bright yellow.

Flower Characteristics: Double, classic blooms.

Plant Characteristics: Grows well in containers and is frequently seen as a miniature tree rose.

New Beginning

Color: Orange-red with yellow at base.

Flower Characteristics: Double, very colorful blooms. Early spring bloom with continuous flowers all season.

Plant Characteristics: Tidy, disease resistant, and winter hardy in all but the coldest regions. This rose grows 16 to 20 inches in height; use as a hedge or in low border. All-America Rose Selections (AARS) winner.

Over the Rainbow

Color: Red blended with yellow.

Flower Characteristics: Bicolor, double blooms measure 1¼ to 1½ inches across and have 28 to 35 petals. Blooms exhibit little fragrance. Midseason bloom with all-

season repeat.

Plant Characteristics: Upright, well branched, disease resistant, and winter hardy. Grows 12 to 14 inches tall; use for beds and borders.

Party Girl

Color: Apricot flushed with pink.

Flower Characteristics: Double, classic hybrid-tea–form blooms measure 1¼ inches across and have 25 petals. Blooms exhibit a rich, spicy fragrance. Midseason bloom with good repeat.

Plant Characteristics: Bushy, upright, compact, disease resistant, and winter hardy. Grows 12 to 15 inches tall and does beautifully in beds, borders, edgings, and containers. Grows well indoors.

Peaches 'n' Cream

Color: Pink and cream blend.

Kathy

Mixed Miniatures border

Flower Characteristics: Double, classic hybrid-tea–form blooms measure 1½ inches across and have 50 petals. Blooms are lightly fragrant and long lasting. Midseason bloom with good repeat.

Plant Characteristics: Upright, disease resistant, and winter hardy. This well-branched rose grows 15 to 18 inches tall and is a good choice for beds and borders. A very reliable performer for rose gardens in any climate.

Popcorn

Color: White.

Flower Characteristics: Creamy white buds open to a single, 5-petaled, cupped bloom that measures ¾ inch across with showy yellow stamens. Blooms in clusters of small flowers that resemble popcorn and has a sweet, honey fragrance. Midseason bloom with excellent repeat.

Plant Characteristics: Vigorous, disease resistant, and winter hardy. This compact rose grows 12 to 14 inches tall and is excellent for beds, borders, edgings, and containers.

Pride 'n' Joy

Color: Orange with yellow reverse.

Flower Characteristics: Shapely buds open to colorful blooms.

Plant Characteristics: Vigorous, compact, and rounded. This bushy rose grows well in containers. All-America Rose

Selections (AARS) winner.

Puppy Love

Color: Orange blended with pale yellow and pink tones.

Flower Characteristics: Double, classic hybrid-tea–form blooms measure 1½ inches across and have 24 to 30 petals. Flowers exhibit little or light fragrance. Midseason bloom with good repeat.

Plant Characteristics: Upright, disease resistant, and winter hardy. This compact rose grows 12 to 15 inches tall and is a good choice for beds, borders, and container gardens.

Rainbow's End

Color: Yellow-orange edged with red.

Flower Characteristics: Pointed buds open to double, classic hybrid-tea–form blooms 1½ inches across with 24 to 30 petals. Blossoms exhibit little or light fragrance. Midseason bloom with good repeat.

Plant Characteristics: Upright, compact, well branched, disease resistant, and winter hardy. This bushy rose grows 14 to 18 inches tall and is excellent for beds, borders, edgings, and containers. Grows well indoors.

Rise 'n' Shine

Color: Medium yellow.

Flower Characteristics: Pointed buds open to double, classic hybrid-tea–form blooms 1½ to 1¾ inches across with 35 petals. Blooms singly or in clusters and exhibits little or no fragrance. Midseason bloom with good repeat.

Plant Characteristics: Upright, well branched, disease resistant (except prone to mildew and black spot), and winter hardy. This bushy rose grows 10 to 15 inches tall and excels in beds, borders, and edgings.

Rosmarin

Color: Light pink and white blend.

Flower Characteristics: Double, cupped blooms measure 1½ inches across and have 35 petals. Blossoms exhibit a light fragrance. Midseason bloom with continuous repeat.

Plant Characteristics: Upright, well branched, disease resistant, and exceptionally winter hardy. Grows 12 to 18 inches tall and is a fine rose for beds,

Pride n Joy

Small Miracle

borders, and edgings. Looks particularly nice planted near blue flowers such as lavender or catmint.

Simplex

Color: White.

Flower Characteristics: Single, flat blooms measure 1¼ inches across and have 5 petals with showy yellow stamens. Blooms in clusters. Midseason bloom with all-season repeat.

Plant Characteristics: Upright, well branched, disease resistant, and exceptionally winter hardy. This rose grows 15 to 18 inches tall and is a good choice for beds and borders. In cool climates, this rose is pale pink. Pinch it back to avoid legginess.

Small Miracle

Color: White tinged with pink.

Flower Characteristics: Double blooms have slightly pointed petals and open flat. Lightly scented.

Plant Characteristics: An excellent choice for containers or window boxes. Works well as a front border to taller roses. Developed and sold by Jackson & Perkins to benefit the Better Homes Foundation for programs helping homeless families.

Snow Bride

Color: Creamy white.

Flower Characteristics: Abundant blooms.

Plant Characteristics: Upright, well branched, disease resistant, and winter hardy. Grows 15 to 18 inches tall and excels in beds and borders.

Starina

Color: Orange-red.

Flower Characteristics: Pointed buds open to double, classic hybrid-tea–form blooms 1½ inches across with 35 petals. Large blossoms exhibit light fragrance. Midseason bloom with all-season repeat.

Plant Characteristics: Upright, bushy, disease resistant, and exceptionally winter hardy. This compact rose grows 12 to 18 inches tall and is an excellant choice for beds, borders, containers, and edgings. Often considered to be the best miniature rose in its color class.

Stars 'n' Stripes

Color: Red and white stripes.

Flower Characteristics: Semidouble, cupped blooms measure 1¾ inches across and have 14 petals. Large blossoms exhibit light fragrance. Midseason bloom with good repeat.

Plant Characteristics: Upright, disease resistant, and exceptionally winter hardy. Canes can reach 36 inches and are very spreading, which make this rose a fine choice for hanging baskets and containers. Most popular striped miniature. Introduced for the U.S. Bicentennial in 1976.

Top Secret

Color: Deep red.

Flower Characteristics: Double, high-centered, fragrant blooms. Profuse all-season bloom.

Plant Characteristics: Upright, vigorous, and small. Sport of 'Beauty Secret.'

Toy Clown

Color: White edged with red.

Flower Characteristics: Semidouble, cupped to flat blooms measure 1½ inches across and have 12 to 20 petals. Blossoms exhibit little or light fragrance. Midseason bloom with good repeat.

Plant Characteristics: Upright, disease resistant, but not always winter hardy in northern climates. This 10- to 14-inch-tall rose spreads easily, which makes it a good choice for hanging baskets, containers, and beds. Grows well indoors.

Willie Winkie

Color: Pink.

Flower Characteristics: Double, small, cupped blooms. Profuse continuous bloom.

Plant Characteristics: Small and vigorous. Relatively disease resistant with dark green foliage.

Yellow Doll

Color: Light yellow.

Flower Characteristics: Double, classic hybrid-tea–form blooms measure 1½ inches across and have 24 to 30 petals. Blossoms exhibit a light scent. Midseason bloom with good repeat.

Plant Characteristics: Low, compact, and bushy. Disease resistant, and winter hardy.

Alfred de Dalmas

This rose grows 8 to 10 inches tall; use it for beds, borders, containers, and edgings. A climbing form is available that reaches 4 feet in height.

OLD GARDEN ROSES

Defined as any rose that has been in cultivation since 1867, old garden roses contain a diverse assortment of voluptuous bloomers. In this group you'll find a rose to fit any garden situation, from low, sprawling bushes to tall, rangy shrubs. Generally, these old-fashioned beauties have glorious, richly fragrant flowers. Although many repeat bloom, others produce blossoms only once in a fantastic show of annual color. Hardiness varies for old garden rose varieties, so check with your local nursery for roses that excel in your area.

Alfred de Dalmas

Color: Light pink maturing to white.

Flower Characteristics: Double, cup-shape blooms measure 2½ to 3 inches across and have 55 to 65 petals. Fragrant blossoms grow in clusters. Midseason bloom with repeat in the fall. The calyx and stems bear a light, brownish moss.

Plant Characteristics: Compact, low, spreading, disease resistant, and winter hardy. This damask moss rose grows 2 to 3 feet tall and has thorny canes. Suitable for low hedges or small gardens. Also called 'Mousseline.'

American Beauty

Color: Pink.

Flower Characteristics: Double blooms measure 5 to 6 inches across and have 50 petals. Intensely fragrant blooms are hybrid tea in form. Midseason bloom with repeat in the fall.

Plant Characteristics: Upright, disease resistant, and winter hardy. This hybrid perpetual grows 4 to 6 feet tall and has smooth and nearly thornless canes. It bears the name 'Madame Ferdinand Jamain' in Europe. A climbing form is available.

Archduke Charles

Color: Pink with white blend matures to red in sunlight.

Flower Characteristics: Double, loose blooms measure 2 to 3 inches across and have 35 to 40 petals. All-season bloom. Color of the flowers intensifies when grown in bright sunlight.

Plant Characteristics: Bushy, moderately disease resistant, but not always winter hardy in northern gardens. Will grow 2 to 3 feet tall with proper care. This China rose has reddish canes with sparsely scattered red thorns.

Austrian Copper

Color: Orange with yellow reverse.

Flower Characteristics: Single, 5-petaled blooms measure 1 inch across and reveal golden stamens. Profuse flowering with no repeat.

Plant Characteristics: Winter hardy in northern gardens. Grows 4 to 5 feet tall. A rose that dates to before 1590. Small, light green leaves cover the arching, medium-thorny canes.

Baron Girod de l'Ain

Color: Medium red edged with a line of white.

Flower Characteristics: Double, cup-shape, and richly fragrant blooms measure 4 inches across and have 35 to 40 petals. Good midseason bloom with fall repeat. When fully opened, outer petals are saucer shaped with inner petals remaining cup shaped. The pronouncement of the white edging varies with the season.

Plant Characteristics: Upright, well branched, disease resistant, and winter hardy. This rose grows 4 to 5 feet tall and produces wonderful cut flowers. The canes are slightly thorny.

Baroness Rothschild

Color: Light pink with darker pink center.

Flower Characteristics: Double, shallowly cupped blooms measure 5 to 6 inches across and have 40 petals. Abundant midseason bloom with fall repeat. Blooms grow singly or in clusters.

Plant Characteristics: Upright, well branched, disease resistant, and winter hardy. This hybrid perpetual rose grows 4 to 6 feet tall. Also known as 'Baronne Adolphe de Rothschild.' Excellent cut flower because of its long-lasting bloom. Makes an excellent specimen plant. The

Austrian Copper

canes have few thorns and glossy green leaves.

Baronne Prévost

Color: Medium pink.

Flower Characteristics: Very double, full, and richly fragrant blooms measure 3 to 4 inches across and have 100 petals. Good midseason bloom with fall repeat. Bloom is full and quartered with a small button center.

Plant Characteristics: Upright, bushy, disease resistant, and winter hardy. This hybrid perpetual grows 4 to 6 feet in height with very thorny canes. A good choice for northern gardens.

Blanc Double de Coubert

Belle de Crécy

Color: Pink maturing to mauve.

Flower Characteristics: Very double, full, and richly fragrant blooms measure 2 to 3 inches across and have 200 petals. Long midseason bloom but is not recurrent. Bloom is full with a green pip at the center. Blooms change color from pink to mauve (and tints in between) so there are frequently many colors on the bush at the same time. Blooms are so heavy the plant may need support.

Plant Characteristics: Upright, rounded, compact, disease resistant, and winter hardy. This gallica rose grows 4 to 5 feet tall with bristly canes. Named for Madame de Pompadour and reportedly was grown in her garden at Crécy.

Blanc Double de Coubert

Color: White.

Flower Characteristics: Semidouble, 18- to 24-petaled, loose blooms measure 2 to 3 inches across. Good early to midseason bloom with all-season repeat. Petals have a paperlike appearance and reveal golden stamens. Exhibits a strong, sweet fragrance.

Plant Characteristics: Upright, disease

resistant, and very winter hardy in northern climates. This popular, fast-growing rugosa shrub rose grows 3 to 6 feet tall and is not a rose for a small garden. A valuable rose for ground covers, hedges, and large beds. Remove spent blossoms to encourage more blooms. In the autumn the plants produce colorful hips that are attractive to songbirds during the winter months.

Blush Noisette

Color: Blush white.

Flower Characteristics: Double, cup-shape, and richly fragrant blooms measure 2 inches across and have 24 petals. Blooms in clusters, midseason with repeat.

Plant Characteristics: Upright, arching, disease resistant, but not always winter hardy in northern climates. This noisette rose grows 5 to 10 feet tall with nearly thornless canes. Suitable for use as a climber on a wall or fence.

Boule de Neige

Color: White.

Flower Characteristics: Pink buds open to white, double blooms that measure 2 to 4 inches across and have 100 petals. Long midseason bloom with good repeat. The blooms are very fragrant, ball-like, and grow in clusters. Appropriately named, 'Boule de Neige' is French for "snowball."

Plant Characteristics: Upright, slender,

disease resistant, and winter hardy. This bourbon rose grows 4 to 5 feet tall and has dark green foliage that offers a striking contrast to this charming white rose.

Camaieux

Color: Blush with pink strips maturing to mauve and white.

Flower Characteristics: Double, cup-shape blooms measure 3 to 4 inches across and have 65 petals. Blooms early to midseason but is not recurrent. The blooms are camellialike and exhibit a sweet, spicy scent.

Plant Characteristics: Upright, rounded, compact, disease resistant (except to mildew in Southern climates), and winter hardy. This gallica rose grows 3 to 5 feet tall. In the autumn the plants produce quantities of colorful hips.

Cardinal de Richelieu

Color: Purple fading to white at the base.

Flower Characteristics: Double, richly fragrant, loose, cup-shape blooms measure 2½ to 3 inches across and have 35 to 45 petals. Blooms midseason but is not recurrent. The darkest of the gallica roses.

Plant Characteristics: Upright, compact, disease resistant, and winter hardy. This rose grows 3 to 4 feet tall and is nearly thornless. An excellent garden shrub because of its arching branches.

Celsiana

Color: Light pink.

Flower Characteristics: Semidouble, intensely fragrant, cup-shape blooms measure 3½ to 4 inches across and have 12 to 18 petals. Wide open blooms expose showy golden stamens. Grows in sprays of bloom. Blooms midseason but is not recurrent. Petals are quite fragrant when dried.

Plant Characteristics: Upright, arching, disease resistant, and winter hardy. This damask rose grows 4 to 5 feet tall. A very old variety that's been in existence since before 1750.

Charles de Mills

Color: Magenta.

Flower Characteristics: Very double, full, and fragrant blooms measure 3 to 3½ inches across and have 200 petals. Midseason bloom but is not recurrent. Blooms are extremely full with swirled petals that are flat across the top. Quite large and spectacular blooms.

Plant Characteristics: Upright, bushy, disease resistant, and winter hardy. This gallica shrub rose grows 4 to 5 feet tall with bristly canes. Although they bloom only once a year, their extraordinary flower show is worth waiting for.

Charles de Mills

richly fragrant blooms measure 3 to 3½ inches across and have 200 petals. Lengthy midseason bloom but is not recurrent. Blooms are extremely full and round.

Plant Characteristics: Upright, arching, disease resistant, and winter hardy. This centifolia rose is not a true moss rose, although the sepals are fringed. Grows 4 to 6 feet tall with bristly and thorny canes. Also known as 'Chapeau de Napoléon' (French for Napoleon's hat, because the bud has the appearance of a three-cornered hat) and Rosa centifolia cristata.

Delicata

Color: Mauve-pink.

Flower Characteristics: Semidouble, 18- to 24-petaled blooms measure 3 to 3½ inches across. Profuse early to midseason bloom with good repeat. Exhibits a fragrant, clove scent.

Plant Characteristics: Upright, well branched, compact, disease resistant, and winter hardy in northern climates. This dense shrub rose is a rugosa, grows 3½ to 4½ feet tall, and has thorny canes. Produces large hips and blooms at the same time.

Duchesse de Brabant

Color: Pink.

Flower Characteristics: Semidouble, cup-shape, 18- to 24-petaled blooms measure 4 to 5 inches across. Profuse early

Common Moss

Color: Pink.

Flower Characteristics: Very double, richly fragrant blooms measure 3 inches across and have 200 petals. Midseason bloom but is not recurrent. Blooms are extremely tightly packed, quartered, with a button center. Calyx and stems bear heavy moss, and sepals are fringed and long.

Plant Characteristics: Upright, arching, disease resistant, and winter hardy. This moss rose grows 5 to 7 feet tall with bristly canes. Also known as 'Communis,' Rosa centifolia muscosa, and 'Old Pink Moss.'

Comte de Chambord

Color: Medium pink to mauve.

Flower Characteristics: Very double blooms measure 3 inches across and have 200 petals. Midseason bloom is followed by good repeat. Blooms are extremely tightly packed and quartered and exhibit a true rose scent.

Plant Characteristics: Upright, compact, disease resistant, and winter hardy. Grows 4 feet tall with moderately thorny canes.

Crested Moss

Color: Medium pink.

Flower Characteristics: Very double,

to midseason bloom with good repeat. Exhibits an intense tea scent.

Plant Characteristics: Upright, bushy, and disease resistant, but not always winter hardy. This tea rose grows 3 to 5 feet tall and has moderately thorny canes.

Eglantine

Color: Deep pink.

Flower Characteristics: Single, apple-scented blooms. Profuse early spring bloom but is not recurrent.

Plant Characteristics: Upright, vigorous, and very winter hardy. Grows 6 to 7 feet

Crested Moss

tall. Produces large colorful hips. Also called 'Sweet Briar' and Rosa eglanteria. Dates to before 1551. Plant in the back of the border where it won't overtake its neighbors.

Empress Josephine

Color: Pink.

Flower Characteristics: Semidouble, 24- to 30-petaled blooms measure 3 to 5 inches across. Midseason bloom but is not recurrent. Exhibits a slight fragrance. Petals are wavy and appear paperlike.

Plant Characteristics: Low, compact, disease resistant, and winter hardy. This gallica rose is a cross between Rosa cinnamomea and Rosa gallica. Grows 3 to 4 feet tall and has smooth, thornless canes. Named for Empress Josephine, wife of Napoleon Bonaparte, it is a tribute to the woman who is responsible for establishing interest in roses in Europe at that time.

F. J. Grootendorst

Color: Crimson.

Flower Characteristics: Clusters of small flowers with frilled petals. The carnationlike flowers exhibit no scent. Continuous bloom.

Plant Characteristics: Upright, and bushy. This rugosa grows to 5 feet tall and has three sports: 'Pink Grootendorst', 'Grootendorst Supreme' (darker crimson), and 'White Grootendorst'.

Fantin-Latour

Color: Pale blush.

Flower Characteristics: Very double, cup-shape, richly fragrant blooms measure 3 to 3½ inches across and have 200 petals. Midseason bloom but is not recurrent. Blooms are extremely full with a button center.

Plant Characteristics: Upright, well branched, disease resistant, and winter hardy. This rose is classified as a centifolia. Grows 4 to 6 feet tall with nearly thornless

F.J. Grootendorst

canes. Named for the French artist Henri Fantin-Latour.

Félicité Parmentier

Color: Light pink.

Flower Characteristics: Tightly packed, 2-inch, quartered blooms open to expose creamy edges. The blooms grow in clusters and are pleasantly fragrant. Abundant bloom but is not recurrent.

Plant Characteristics: Bushy, low, and grows 4 to 5 feet. This alba rose has very thorny canes.

Ferdinand Pichard

Color: Red and pink or white striped.

Flower Characteristics: Double, cup-shape blooms are 3 to 3½ inches across and have 25 petals. Pink roses have stripes and splashes of red. The pink fades to white as the bloom matures. Good midseason bloom with intermittent repeat. Fragrant blooms.

Plant Characteristics: Upright and compact. Disease resistant, and winter hardy. This hybrid perpetual rose grows 4 to 6 feet tall and has nearly thornless canes. An excellent small garden rose, it is considered one of the best striped roses.

Frau Karl Druschki

Color: White.

Flower Characteristics: Double, classic hybrid-tea–form blooms are 4 to 4½ inches across and have 35 petals. Good midseason bloom with fall repeat. Blossoms exhibit little or light fragrance. The white bloom has a hint of yellow.

Plant Characteristics: Upright, well branched, disease resistant, and winter hardy. This hybrid perpetual and hybrid tea cross grows 4 to 7 feet tall with nearly thornless canes. Also called 'Reine des Neiges,' 'Snow Queen,' and 'White American Beauty.' An excellent rose for the back of a border.

Gloire de Dijon

Color: Yellow blending to orange at center.

Flower Characteristics: Double, classic hybrid-tea–form blooms are 4 inches across and have 45 to 55 petals. Good early season bloom with following repeat bloom. Flowers exhibit a pleasant fragrance.

Plant Characteristics: Upright, arching, disease resistant, and moderately winter hardy. This climbing tea rose is an excellent choice for pillars and walls and grows 10 to 20 feet tall.

Grüss an Aachen

Color: Light pink maturing to creamy white.

Flower Characteristics: Large, cup-shape blooms are full petaled, measure 3 to 5 inches, and exhibit a rich fragrance. Profuse bloom with excellent repeat.

Plant Characteristics: Spreading, disease resistant, and winter hardy. This floribunda was developed in 1909 and grows 2 to 3 feet tall. A good choice for hedges.

Grüss an Teplitz

Color: Medium red.

Flower Characteristics: Double, cup-shape blooms are 3 to 3½ inches across and have 34 to 40 petals. Abundant midseason bloom with good repeat. Spicy fragrance.

Plant Characteristics: Upright, arching, disease resistant, and winter hardy except in very cold climates. This hybrid China rose can grow 3 to 6 feet in height.

Hansa

Color: Red-violet.

Flower Characteristics: Double, cup-shape blooms have 35 to 40 petals and measure 3 to 3½ inches across. Profuse early to midseason bloom with good repeat. The loose blooms exhibit a fragrant, clove scent.

Plant Characteristics: Upright, bushy, disease resistant, and winter hardy. This dense shrub rose is a rugosa, grows 4 to 5 feet tall, and has thorny canes.

Harison's Yellow

Color: Deep yellow.

Flower Characteristics: Double, cup-shape blooms have 20 to 24 petals and measure 2 to 2½ inches across. Profuse early season bloom but is not recurrent. Blooms along the length of long canes. Flowers have showy yellow stamens.

Plant Characteristics: Upright, spreading, arching, disease resistant, and winter hardy. This popular shrub rose has attractive, ferny foliage and grows 5 to 7 feet tall.

Henri Martin

Color: Dark red.

Flower Characteristics: Double, round blooms have 65 to 75 petals and measure 2½ inches across. Profuse mid- to late-season bloom and is not recurrent. Calyx and sepals bear heavy moss. Blooms are richly fragrant. Blooms are borne on slender, wiry stems.

Plant Characteristics: Upright, arching, disease resistant, and winter hardy. This moss rose has thorny canes and grows 5 to 6 feet tall.

Henry Nevard

Color: Deep red.

Flower Characteristics: Double, cup-shape blooms have 30 petals and measure 4 to 4½ inches across. Profuse midseason bloom with good repeat. Blooms are richly fragrant. Blooms are borne on long stems.

Plant Characteristics: Upright, bushy, disease resistant, and winter hardy in northern gardens. This hybrid perpetual

grows 4 to 5 feet tall.

Ispahan

Color: Medium pink.

Flower Characteristics: Double, cup-shape, loose blooms have 24 to 30 petals and measure 2½ to 3 inches across. Profuse and lengthy early to midseason bloom but is not recurrent. Blooms open flat and are intensely fragrant.

Plant Characteristics: Upright, bushy, disease resistant, and winter hardy. This shrub rose is classed as a damask, has thorny canes, and grows 4 to 6 feet tall. Also called 'Pompon des Princes.'

Jacques Cartier

Color: Pink.

Flower Characteristics: Very double, cup-shape blooms measure 3 to 4 inches across and have 200 petals. Profuse bloom with fair repeat. The loose blooms open to button center. Very fragrant.

Plant Characteristics: Upright, compact, disease resistant, and winter hardy. This rose grows 2 to 4 feet tall.

Königin von Dänemark

Color: Light pink with deep pink center.

Flower Characteristics: Very double, intensely fragrant blooms have 200 petals and measure 3½ inches across. Profuse early season bloom, but is not recurrent.

Blooms are cup shaped and quartered with button center.

Plant Characteristics: Upright and slender. Disease resistant and winter hardy. This alba has thorny canes and grows 4 to 6 feet tall. It was raised as a seedling of 'Maiden's Blush.' Also called 'Queen of Denmark.'

La Reine Victoria

Color: Medium pink.

Flower Characteristics: Double, intensely fragrant, cup-shape blooms have 35 petals and measure 3 to 3½ inches across. Abundant midseason bloom with good fall repeat.

Plant Characteristics: Upright, slender, disease resistant, and winter hardy. This bourbon rose has smooth, nearly thornless canes and grows 4 to 6 feet tall.

La Ville de Bruxelles

Color: Medium to deep pink.

Flower Characteristics: Double, intensely fragrant blooms have 45 to 55 petals and measure 4 to 5 inches across. Abundant midseason bloom but is not recurrent. Heavy blooms are quartered with a green button center.

Plant Characteristics: Upright, bushy, disease resistant, and relatively winter hardy in northern gardens. This damask rose has weighty, full blooms borne on moderately thorny canes and grows 4 to 7 feet tall. Foliage is light green and glossy.

Louise Odier

Color: Medium pink.

Flower Characteristics: Double, intensely fragrant blooms have 35 to 45 petals and measure 3½ inches across. Abundant midseason bloom with good repeat. Blooms open to be cup shaped, then are flatter, quartered, and full.

Plant Characteristics: Upright, slender, disease resistant, and winter hardy in northern climates. This bourbon rose has smooth canes and grows 4½ to 5½ feet tall. A favorite rose of Victorian gardeners and a reliable recurrent bloomer.

Mabel Morrison

Color: White.

Flower Characteristics: Double,

Old roses in a driveway border

shallowly cupped blooms have 30 petals and measure 3½ to 4 inches across. Midseason bloom with good fall repeat. Blooms exhibit little or light fragrance. In cooler weather this rose takes on a light blush.

Plant Characteristics: Upright, well branched, disease resistant, and winter hardy. This hybrid perpetual has thorny canes and grows 3 to 4½ feet tall. A white sport of 'Baroness Rothschild.' The compact growth habit of this rose makes it a good choice for small gardens.

Madame Alfred Carrière

Color: White.

Flower Characteristics: Double, gardenia-shape blooms have 35 petals and measure 3 to 4 inches across. Midseason bloom with good repeat. Blooms are fragrant and grow in clusters.

Plant Characteristics: Upright and arching. Disease resistant, but not always winter hardy in colder climates. This rose has thorny canes and grows 8 to 15 feet tall. It is a suitable rose for arches, pergolas, walls, and pillars, but it also can grow as a shrub. As a climber, it will tolerate shade.

Madame Hardy

Color: White.

Flower Characteristics: Very double, full, and lemon-scented blooms measure 3 to 3½ inches across and have 200 petals. Midseason bloom but is not recurrent. Blooms open to cupped shape, and then are flat with a green pip in the center.

Plant Characteristics: Upright, bushy, disease resistant, and winter hardy. This popular white rose grows 4 to 6 feet tall with moderately thorny canes. Classified as a damask. Bred in 1832, it makes an excellent specimen plant or barrier hedge.

Madame Isaac Pereire

Color: Deep pink.

Flower Characteristics: Double, full, round, and richly fragrant blooms measure 4 to 5 inches across and have 45 to 55 petals. Abundant midseason bloom with excellent fall repeat. Blooms are extremely full and quartered.

Plant Characteristics: Upright, bushy, spreading, disease resistant, and winter hardy in northern rose gardens. This bourbon rose is favored for its intense fragrance and grows 4 to 7 feet tall with moderately thorny canes. Foliage is dark and shiny green.

Madame Legras de St. Germain

Color: White with yellow center.

Flower Characteristics: Very double, full, and sweetly fragrant blooms measure

3½ inches across and have 200 petals. Early and lengthy bloom but is not recurrent. Blooms are extremely full with a green pip in the center. Flowers do not hold up well in wet weather.

Plant Characteristics: Upright, arching, disease resistant, and winter hardy. This alba grows 6 to 12 feet tall with smooth, thornless canes.

Madame Louis Lévêque

Color: Light pink.

Flower Characteristics: Double, full, round, and richly fragrant blooms measure 3 to 3½ inches across and have 100 petals. Abundant midseason bloom with fall repeat. Blooms are extremely full. Lightly mossed.

Plant Characteristics: Upright, arching, disease resistant, and winter hardy. This hybrid moss rose grows 4 to 5 feet tall. Blooms are borne on thorny canes.

Madame Pierre Oger

Color: Pale blush.

Flower Characteristics: Double, cup-shape blooms measure 3 to 3½ inches across and have 35 petals. Abundant midseason bloom with fall repeat. Blooms are extremely fragrant and deepen in color when exposed to sunlight.

Plant Characteristics: Upright, slender, disease resistant, and winter hardy in northern gardens. This bourbon rose grows 4½ to 6 feet tall. Blooms are borne on smooth, nearly thornless canes. A color sport of 'La Reine Victoria.' A popular selection with Victorian rose gardeners.

Madame Plantier

Color: White.

Flower Characteristics: Very double, full, clustered blooms measure 2½ to 3 inches across and have 200 petals. Abundant midseason bloom but is not recurrent. Blooms are extremely fragrant and have a button center with a green eye. Bush is covered with large clusters of pomponlike blooms.

Plant Characteristics: Sprawling, dense, bushy, disease resistant, and winter hardy. Grows 5 to 6 feet tall and wide with smooth, nearly thornless canes. Can be trained as a climber onto a trellis or a tree.

Maiden's Blush

Color: Light pink.

Flower Characteristics: Very double, full blooms measure 2½ to 3 inches across and have 200 petals. Abundant early to midseason bloom but is not recurrent. Blooms are extremely fragrant and very full with a muddled center.

Plant Characteristics: Upright, treelike, then arching. Disease resistant, and winter hardy. This alba grows 4 to 6 feet tall with

bristly, thorny canes. A very old rose, it was cultivated before 1600. 'Small Maiden's Blush,' an identical but smaller version, grows 4 feet tall.

Maman Cochet

Color: Light pink with yellow base.

Flower Characteristics: Double, hybrid-tea–form blooms are 3½ to 4 inches across and have 35 to 45 petals. Abundant midseason bloom with good repeat. Blooms exhibit a nice fragrance. Color deepens in the sunlight.

Plant Characteristics: Upright, bushy, and disease resistant, but not winter hardy in northern climates. This popular tea rose grows 3 to 4 feet tall with smooth, nearly thornless canes. A white climbing form called 'White Madame Cochet' also is available.

Marchioness of Londonderry

Color: Light pink.

Flower Characteristics: Double, round blooms are 4½ to 5 inches across and have 50 petals. Abundant midseason bloom with fair repeat. Blooms are full and exhibit a strong fragrance.

Plant Characteristics: Upright, arching, disease resistant but not winter hardy in most northern climates. This hybrid perpetual rose grows 5 to 7 feet tall and has

smooth, nearly thornless canes. It is a good addition for rose gardens located in mild climates.

Maréchal Niel

Color: Yellow.

Flower Characteristics: Large, very double blooms exhibit a light fragrance. Abundant bloom with good repeat.

Plant Characteristics: Upright and not always winter hardy. This noisette rose grows 10 feet tall. Suitable for walls and fences.

May Queen

Color: Light pink.

Flower Characteristics: Double, round blooms are 4 to 5 inches across and have 45 to 55 petals. Abundant, lengthy midseason bloom. Blooms are fragrant, quartered, and have a button center.

Plant Characteristics: Upright, arching, disease resistant, and winter hardy in northern climates. Under good growing conditions this climbing rose will grow 15 to 25 feet tall. The foliage is medium green and glossy.

Musk Rose

Color: White.

Flower Characteristics: Single, 5-petaled, 1½-inch blooms expose yellow stamens. One annual flowering.

Plant Characteristics: Grows 20 to 30 feet. This rose is mentioned in the works of Shakespeare. This ancient rose is also called Rosa moschata.

Mutabilis

Color: Deep pink

Flower Characteristics: Copper-red buds open to single, 5-petaled, 3-inch pink blooms that mature to deep pink. Consistent bloom. Very fragrant.

Plant Characteristics: Upright and not consistently winter hardy. Does best in a

Maréchal Niel

warm, protected area and will grow 3 to 6 feet tall. Species rose is also called Rosa chinensis mutabilis.

Old Blush

Color: Medium pink

Flower Characteristics: Double, cup-shape blooms are 3 inches across and have 24 to 30 petals. Abundant all-season bloom. Blooms have little or light fragrance, are loosely formed, and grow in clusters.

Plant Characteristics: Upright, bushy, and disease resistant but not winter hardy. This China rose grows 3 to 5 feet tall with smooth, nearly thornless canes.

Paul Neyron

Color: Medium to deep pink.

Flower Characteristics: Very double, full blooms measure 4½ to 5½ inches across and have 65 to 75 petals. Midseason bloom with fall repeat. Blooms are extremely fragrant and very full with a muddled center, sometimes quartered.

Plant Characteristics: Upright, arching, disease resistant, and winter hardy in northern gardens. This hybrid perpetual grows 5 to 6 feet tall with smooth, nearly thornless canes.

Pax

Color: Ivory.

Flower Characteristics: Semidouble, 4-inch blooms are very fragrant and are borne on long stems. Excellent all-season bloom.

Plant Characteristics: Disease resistant and winter hardy. Grows 6 to 8 feet tall and does well in filtered light. This hybrid musk rose is suitable for training on an arbor or along a fence.

Penelope

Color: Pale salmon, almost white.

Flower Characteristics: Semidouble blooms have 18 to 24 petals. Produces flowers midseason with good repeat. Blossoms grow in clusters, are fragrant and cup shaped, and have bright yellow stamens.

Plant Characteristics: Upright, bushy, disease resistant, and winter hardy. A good choice for a hedge. This hybrid musk shrub rose also produces greenish-pink hips in autumn.

Petite de Hollande

Color: Medium pink.

Flower Characteristics: Double, full, round blooms measure 2 to 2½ inches across and have 45 to 55 petals. Midseason bloom is abundant and lengthy but is not recurrent. Blooms are extremely fragrant.

Plant Characteristics: Upright, bushy, disease resistant, and winter hardy. This small centifolia shrub grows 3½ to 4 feet

tall and is an excellent choice for small gardens because of its miniature blooms and leaves.

Prosperity

Color: Ivory with yellow at the base.

Flower Characteristics: Double, 1½-inch blooms grow in graceful compact clusters. Abundant all-season bloom.

Plant Characteristics: Grows to 4 feet tall. This hybrid musk is suitable as a hedge.

Reine des Violettes

Color: Mauve.

Flower Characteristics: Very double, cup-shape, and richly fragrant blooms measure 3 inches across and have 70 to 75 petals. Blooms open flat and are quartered with a button center. Abundant midseason bloom with occasional fall repeat. The color of this rose changes from mauve to lavender.

Plant Characteristics: Upright, bushy, disease resistant, and winter hardy in northern climates. This hybrid perpetual grows 5 to 8 feet tall with smooth canes. 'Reine des Violettes' is French for the Queen of Violets. Often considered the best of the repeat flowering roses of its color.

Rêve d'Or

Color: Yellow.

Reine des Violettes

Flower Characteristics: Blooms begin as buff yellow and fade to lighter yellow as the flower matures. Abundant early season bloom with intermittent repeat.

Plant Characteristics: Vigorous. This noisette rose grows 10 to 12 feet tall.

Rosa damascena bifera

Color: Pink.

Flower Characteristics: Very double, 3½-inch-wide blooms are intensely fragrant and grow in clusters. Good all-season bloom.

Plant Characteristics: This ancient rose grows to 3 to 4 feet tall.

Rosa gallica officinalis

Color: Medium to deep pink.

Flower Characteristics: Semidouble, cup-shape, and richly fragrant blooms measure 3 to 3½ inches across and have 12 to 24 petals. Abundant midseason bloom but is not recurrent. Blooms have showy yellow stamens and are quite fragrant when dried.

Plant Characteristics: Low, branching, compact, disease resistant, and winter hardy. This ancient rose grows 3 to 4 feet tall and is suitable for borders, low hedges, or ground covers. Also called the 'Apothecary Rose,' this rose was used for

Penelope

centuries for medicinal purposes. It was dried, sugared, and infused into syrups that were used as remedies for a number of ailments.

Also widely used in the production of perfume. This gallica rose is reported to be the Red Rose of Lancaster, the rose emblem selected by the House of Lancaster during the Wars of the Roses.

Rosa hugonis

Color: Pale yellow.

Flower Characteristics: Single, cup-shape blooms measure 1 to 2½ inches across and have 5 petals. Very early, abundant bloom but is not recurrent. Blooms have showy golden stamens. Little or light fragrance.

Plant Characteristics: Upright, arching, disease resistant, and winter hardy except in colder climates. This species rose grows 6 feet tall.

Rosa moschata plena

Color: Ivory.

Flower Characteristics: Double,

Mixed Border

exotically perfumed blooms. Produces abundant and lengthy midseason bloom with no repeat.

Plant Characteristics: Climbing. The double musk rose grows 10 to 20 feet tall. This rose's large thorns enable it to climb trees and arbors with ease. It is an ancient rose that is still popular with modern gardeners.

Rosa Mundi

Color: Pink and white striped.

Flower Characteristics: Semidouble, cup-shape blooms measure 3 to 3½ inches across and have 18 to 24 petals. Abundant midseason bloom but is not recurrent. Blooms have showy golden stamens. The earliest blooming and oldest of the striped roses, each bloom is unique.

Plant Characteristics: Low, sprawling, compact, disease resistant, and winter hardy. This rose grows 3½ to 4 feet wide and tall and is the striped sport of Rosa gallica officinalis. Suitable for low hedges or borders. This gallica rose dates to the 16th century. In late summer the plants develope bright red hips attractive to songbirds.

Rosa rugosa alba

Color: White.

Flower Characteristics: Long, slender buds open to large, 4-inch, single blooms. Continuous all-season bloom. Blooms reveal stamens and are lightly fragrant.

Plant Characteristics: Shrublike, compact, disease resistant, and winter hardy. Grows 3 to 6 feet tall. This rugosa species rose is excellent for massed landscape plantings. Canes are thorny. In the autumn the plants produce colorful hips that are attractive to birds.

Rosa rugosa rubra

Color: Mauve-pink with yellow stamens.

Flower Characteristics: Large, 5-petaled, single blooms measure 3½ inches across and have yellow stamens. Fragrant blooms are produced at the same time as large scarlet hips. Good all-season bloom.

Plant Characteristics: Shrublike with dense green, typically disease-resistant foliage. This rugosa rose is slightly more vigorous than the alba and is arching in growth habit. Grows 4 to 5 feet tall.

Rosa soulieana

Color: White.

Flower Characteristics: Single, 5-petaled, 1½ inch blooms grow in clusters. Heavily perfumed. Blooms are abundant early to midseason with intermittent repeat.

Plant Characteristics: Not reliably winter hardy. This species rose grows 15 to 20 feet tall and produces tiny orange-red hips later in the season. The canes are thorny.

Rose de Rescht

Color: Deep pink.

Flower Characteristics: Very double, full blooms measure 2 to 2½ inches across and have 100 petals. Abundant midseason bloom with good repeat. Blooms are closely packed and intensely fragrant.

Plant Characteristics: Bushy, compact, disease resistant, and winter hardy. This rose grows 2 to 3 feet tall. It reportedly was brought to England from Persia.

Rose du Roi

Color: Medium pink to purple.

Flower Characteristics: Double, loose blooms measure 2½ inches across and have 100 petals. Abundant midseason bloom with good repeat. Blooms are intensely fragrant.

Plant Characteristics: Spreading, compact, disease resistant, and winter hardy. This rose grows 3 to 4 feet tall. 'Rose du Roi' is French for Rose of the King.

Rosette Delizy

Color: Yellow with apricot reverse.

Flower Characteristics: Pointed buds

Rosa Mundi

open to double, hybrid-tea–form blooms that measure 3½ to 4 inches across and have 45 to 55 petals. Abundant midseason bloom with good repeat.

Plant Characteristics: Upright, bushy, and disease resistant, but is not winter hardy. This tea rose grows 3 to 5 feet tall. The canes are relatively thornless.

Salet

Color: Medium pink.

Flower Characteristics: Double, round blooms measure 2½ to 3 inches across and have 55 to 65 petals. Produces abundant midseason bloom with fair fall repeat. Blooms are fragrant. Calyx and sepals are well mossed.

Plant Characteristics: Upright, arching, disease resistant, and winter hardy. This moss rose grows 3 to 5 feet tall.

Seven Sisters

Color: Pink

Flower Characteristics: Named for its varying shades of color (from pink to white) within each cluster of blooms. Prolific bloom midsummer.

Plant Characteristics: A rambler that grows well trained to a fence. Also called 'Rosa platyphylla.'

Sombreuil

Color: White.

Flower Characteristics: Very double, cup-shape blooms are 3½ to 4 inches across with 100 petals. Early to midseason bloom with all-season repeat. Blooms are fragrant and quartered.

Plant Characteristics: Upright, and disease resistant but not always winter hardy. This climbing tea rose is suitable for arches, pergolas, walls, and pillars and grows 5 to 12 feet tall. Will tolerate shade, but needs a warm, sheltered site. Also will grow as a shrub.

Souvenir de la Malmaison

Color: Light pink.

Flower Characteristics: Very double, full, quartered blooms are 4½ to 5 inches across with 65 to 75 petals. Mid- to late-season bloom with reliable repeat. Blooms are cup shaped, becoming flat, and exhibit a spicy scent.

Plant Characteristics: Compact, small, and disease resistant. Bush form reaches 2 to 3 feet; climbing form reaches 6 to 8 feet. Climbing form is suitable for low wooden trellises and pillars. The foliage is medium green and glossy. This bourbon rose is named for the rose garden maintained by Empress Josephine, wife of Napoleon Bonaparte. Malmaison, outside Paris. The garden contained the largest collection of roses of its time.

Striped Moss

Color: Red and white striped.

Flower Characteristics: Double, cup-shape blooms are 1½ to 2 inches across with 45 to 65 petals. Profuse midseason bloom but no repeat. Color fades in bright sunlight to blooms that are pink and white striped. Blooms are fragrant and very packed. Lightly mossed.

Plant Characteristics: Upright, bushy, disease resistant, and winter hardy in northern climates. Reaches 5 to 6 feet tall with very thorny canes.

Thérèse Bugnet

Color: Pink.

Flower Characteristics: Large, intensely fragrant blooms. Prolific bloom from late spring to late summer. Petals resemble tissue paper.

Plant Characteristics: Upright and fountainlike bush. Disease resistant and winter hardy.

Tour de Malakoff

Color: Mauve.

Flower Characteristics: Double, cup-shape, loose blooms measure 3 to 3½ inches across with 45 to 55 petals. Profuse midseason bloom, but no repeat. Color deepens to violet as blooms mature. Blooms are very fragrant.

Plant Characteristics: Upright,

sprawling, disease resistant, and winter hardy. This centifolia reaches 3 to 6 feet in height and has very thorny canes. With suitable support it can be trained as a climber.

Tuscany Superb

Color: Purple.

Flower Characteristics: Double, cup-shape blooms have 24 to 30 petals and measure 3½ to 4 inches across. Profuse midseason bloom, but no repeat. Blooms are well filled, tending to hide bright yellow stamens. A richly fragrant rose.

Plant Characteristics: Upright, compact, disease resistant, and winter hardy. This gallica rose has bristly canes and grows 3 to 4 feet tall. A larger and more vigorous version of Tuscany.

Variegata di Bologna

Color: Red and white striped.

Flower Characteristics: Double, round blooms have 45 to 55 petals and measure 3½ to 4 inches across. Profuse midseason bloom, with occasional repeat. Blooms are cup shaped, quartered, and fragrant. Grows in clusters.

Plant Characteristics: Upright, slender, disease resistant (except to black spot), and winter hardy. This bourbon rose has smooth canes and grows 5 to 8 feet tall. Suitable for trellises and pillars.

White Rose of York

Color: White.

Flower Characteristics: Double, fragrant blooms. Midseason bloom with no repeat.

Plant Characteristics: This alba grows 6 to 8 feet tall. Suitable for back of a bed or as a hedge. This rose is the emblem of the House of York during the Wars of the Roses and dates to before 1597.

Yellow Banksiae

Color: Yellow.

Flower Characteristics: Small, very double blooms in clusters. Early spring bloom.

Plant Characteristics: Vigorous, and tremendous grower. Nearly thornless.

York and Lancaster

Color: Pink and white.

Flower Characteristics: Double, cup-shape blooms have 24 to 30 petals and measure 2½ to 3 inches across. Abundant midseason bloom, but no repeat. Blooms are borne in sprays and are fragrant and loose. When open, bright stamens are exposed.

Plant Characteristics: Bushy; not very vigorous, disease resistant, or winter hardy. This damask rose, which grows 3 to 5 feet tall, dates to 1551, when it was named for the warring houses of England. The Yorks were represented by a white rose; the

Lancasters were represented by a red rose. This rose represents both houses with an intermixing of pink and white petals on the same bloom. The bush also will have exclusively white or pink blooms, but they are evenly split so both colors are represented. The canes are very thorny and the foliage is light green.

Zéphirine Drouhin

Color: Medium pink.

Flower Characteristics: Semidouble, cup-shape blooms have 20 to 24 petals and measure 3½ to 4 inches across. Abundant all-season bloom. Blooms are fragrant and loose.

Plant Characteristics: Upright, vigorous, disease resistant (except prone to black spot and mildew), and winter hardy. This bourbon rose grows 8 to 12 feet tall and is a good low to medium climber. Canes are smooth wood. Essentially a thornless rose. Suitable as large shrub or small climber.

SHRUB/LANDSCAPE

Versatile and hardworking, the shrub and landscape rose group contains classic varieties as well as new hybrids. Used singly or planted in mass, shrub and landscape roses are ideal for solving tough landscaping problems. Low-growing types work well as ground covers and will carpet an area with bloom. Use larger types as

Belinda

specimens, hedges, or screens. Many are extremely winter hardy and produce exceptional blooms with each succeeding season.

Alba Meidiland

Color: White.

Flower Characteristics: Double blooms grow in heavy clusters. Lightly fragrant, they bloom continuously all season.

Plant Characteristics: Dense and spreading, this rose can be used as a ground cover and as a hedge. The blooms also are good for cutting.

All That Jazz

Color: Coral.

Flower Characteristics: Semidouble, 13-petaled, luminous blooms grow in clusters. Lightly scented. Profuse all-season bloom.

Plant Characteristics: Vigorous, hardy, and disease resistant. All-America Rose Selections (AARS) winner.

Amiga Mia

Color: Light pink.

Flower Characteristics: Semidouble, blooms. Abundant all-season bloom. Blooms are fragrant and grow in clusters of 6 to 8, but also grow as singles.

Plant Characteristics: Upright, vigorous, disease resistant, and winter hardy. This shrub grandiflora grows 3 to 5 feet tall. Use

in the back of the border.

Ballerina

Color: Pink flowers with a white center.

Flower Characteristics: Single, 5-petaled, phloxlike blooms measure 2 inches across and grow in large clusters. Bright yellow stamens darken quickly. Midseason bloom with good repeat. Exhibits a slightly musky fragrance.

Plant Characteristics: Arching, disease resistant, and winter hardy. This low-growing, dense shrub rose grows 2 to 4 feet tall and wide and has smooth canes with sparsely scattered thorns. Suitable for hedges.

Belinda

Color: Medium pink.

Flower Characteristics: Semidouble, 12- to 15-petaled blooms measure 1 inch across and grow in large clusters. Midseason bloom with good repeat. Exhibits a light fragrance.

Plant Characteristics: Upright, bushy, disease resistant, and winter hardy. This dense hybrid musk shrub rose grows 4 to 6 feet tall and is an excellent choice for a hedge or a pillar. Grows in light shade.

Bonica

Color: Pink.

Flower Characteristics: Small buds open

to loose, ruffled double blooms with 25 to 30 petals. Color deepens in center of bloom. Lightly fragrant. Grows in clusters. Continuous bloom all season.

Plant Characteristics: Spreading, arching, disease resistant, and very hardy. Plant produces orange hips. This floribunda shrub rose is an ideal choice for a hedge or in mass along a walk or drive. It grows 3 to 4 feet tall and will spread 6 feet wide. All-America Rose Selections (AARS) winner.

Canterbury

Color: Rose-pink.

Flower Characteristics: Semidouble blooms have 10 to 12 petals and reveal golden stamens. Abundant all-season bloom. Blooms are very fragrant.

Plant Characteristics: This shrub rose grows 3 to 5 feet tall and was hybridized by David Austin. Suitable for hedges.

Carefree Beauty

Color: Medium pink.

Flower Characteristics: Semidouble blooms have 15 to 20 petals and are richly fragrant. Grows in clusters of 3 to 20 blooms. Excellent all-season bloom.

Plant Characteristics: Vigorous, bushy, and wide. This floribunda shrub rose grows 4 to 5 feet tall and is a good choice for hedges and ground covers. To create a solid hedge of bloom space plants 18 inches

Carefree Wonder

apart. Generally winter hardy in all climates.

Carefree Wonder

Color: Pink with cream reverse.

Flower Characteristics: Double, loose, 4-inch blooms expose yellow stamens. Lightly fragrant. Very abundant and profuse bloom.

Plant Characteristics: Disease resistant and winter hardy. An excellent shrub rose. All-America Rose Selections (AARS) winner.

Country Dancer

Color: Deep pink to rosy red.

Flower Characteristics: Double blooms have flaring petals that surround stamens. This rose's floribunda heritage makes it ever-blooming. Very fragrant.

Plant Characteristics: Disease resistant,

Bonica

upright, and bushy. Glossy, dark green foliage. Grows 2 to 4 feet tall and is suitable as a hedge.

Earth Song

Color: Deep pink flushed with copper.

Flower Characteristics: Long pointed buds open to cup-shape and fragrant blooms. Grows in clusters of 6 to 8 flowers. Its grandiflora heritage ensures abundant all-season bloom.

Plant Characteristics: Bushy, upright, and disease resistant. Hybrid of 'Music Maker' and 'Prairie Star.' Grows 4 to 5 feet tall and is an excellent shrub rose.

English Garden

Color: Yellow.

Flower Characteristics: Very double, cup-shape blooms. An old rose look with abundant repeat bloom. The color deepens toward the center of the bloom. Continuous bloom throughout the summer.

Plant Characteristics: Upright and compact growth. Grows 3 to 4 feet tall. This elegant English rose was hybridized by David Austin and is an excellent choice for a hedge.

Fair Bianca

Color: White.

Flower Characteristics: Very double, shallowly cupped blooms are heavily

Shrub/Landscape

scented and have a green center. An old rose look with repeat bloom.

Plant Characteristics: Vigorous and upright. Grows 3 to 4 feet tall. A lovely English rose hybridized by David Austin. Excels in beds or as a hedge.

Fritz Nobis

Color: Light pink

Flower Characteristics: Double, slightly ruffled petals open to a hybrid-tea-shaped bloom that exposes golden stamens. Produces clusters of fragrant blooms only once, in early summer.

Plant Characteristics: Large, broad bush has a sprawling growth habit. Produces bright orange hips in autumn. Very vigorous.

Gertrude Jekyll

Color: Pink.

Flower Characteristics: Double, full-petaled blooms are heavily scented with the true damask rose fragrance. An old rose look with repeat bloom.

Plant Characteristics: Vigorous and upright. Grows 4 to 5 feet tall. Named for the renowned English gardener, Gertrude Jekyll. Excellent as a border or hedge.

Graham Thomas

Color: Yellow.

Flower Characteristics: Very double,

cup-shape blooms are strongly tea scented. An old rose look with abundant repeat bloom. Color gradually deepens at the center of the bloom.

Plant Characteristics: Vigorous, bushy, and upright. Grows 4 to 5 feet tall. Named for the influential English rosarian Graham Thomas. This arching English rose was hybridized by David Austin.

Hawkeye Belle

Color: White blushed with pink.

Flower Characteristics: Pointed buds open to flat, double blooms. Grows in clusters or as a single. Color deepens as the bloom matures. Intensely fragrant. As befits its grandiflora heritage, this rose flowers repeatedly.

Plant Characteristics: Upright, bushy, and vigorous. Grows 4 feet tall.

Marie Bugnet

Color: White.

Flower Characteristics: Double, fragrant blooms with flaring petals grow in clusters. Early season bloom with good repeat.

Plant Characteristics: Compact, bushy, and winter hardy. Grows 3 to 4 feet tall and is an excellent hedge rose.

Mary Rose

Color: Pink

Flower Characteristics: Round buds open to very double, 4- to 5-inch fragrant

blooms. Produces abundant blooms early in the season and continues with good repeat.

Plant Characteristics: Grows 4 feet tall and is a very neat shrub. Very vigorous and disease resistant.

Maytime

Color: Apricot with yellow base.

Flower Characteristics: Semidouble, cup-shape blooms have 6 to 10 petals and measure 4 inches across. Fragrant blooms grow in clusters. This rose's floribunda heritage ensures abundant all-season bloom.

Plant Characteristics: Bushy, upright, and winter hardy. Grows 2 to 4 feet tall.

Music Maker

Color: Pink.

Flower Characteristics: Double, fragrant blooms. Grows in clusters and blooms abundantly all season long. Especially long-lived blooms.

Plant Characteristics: Vigorous and disease resistant. Grows 2 to 3 feet tall and wide.

Nymphenburg

Color: Light orange-yellow flushed with pink.

Flower Characteristics: Large, semidouble, scented blooms measure 3½ inches across. Excellent all-season bloom.

Fritz Nobis

Scarlet Meidiland

Grows in compact clusters and is pleasantly scented.

Plant Characteristics: Upright and bushy. Glossy, green foliage. Suitable as a pillar, shrub rose, or hedge. Grows 6 feet tall.

Othello

Color: Dark crimson.

Flower Characteristics: Very double, full-petaled blooms are richly scented. The color changes to tints of purple as the bloom matures. A beautiful old rose look with all-season bloom.

Plant Characteristics: Vigorous, upright, and bushy. This English rose grows 4 to 5 feet tall.

Pink Meidiland

Color: Pink.

Flower Characteristics: Clusters of single blooms. All-season bloom.

Plant Characteristics: Upright. An excellent choice for low hedges or borders.

Prairie Fire

Color: Red.

Flower Characteristics: Double, fragrant blooms measure 3 inches across and have 40 petals. Profuse bloom with good repeat.

Plant Characteristics: Upright and nearly always blooming.

Prairie Flower

Color: Deep pink with a white base.

Flower Characteristics: Single, fragrant blooms are borne on long stems and grow in clusters. The white base highlights bright yellow stamens.

Plant Characteristics: Upright and very winter hardy. Will grow 4 to 6 feet tall under good conditions.

Red Simplicity

Color: Red.

Flower Characteristics: Double blooms grow in clusters. Profuse all-season bloom.

Plant Characteristics: Vigorous and disease resistant. It can grow 3 to 4 feet tall, so it makes an excellent privacy screen.

Sally Holmes

Color: Ivory white.

Flower Characteristics: Single, 3½-inch blooms are fragrant and grow in compact clusters. Good abundant bloom with repeat. Lightly fragrant.

Plant Characteristics: Vigorous and extremely bushy. The dark, shiny green foliage beautifully offsets the white flowers. Grows 4 to 5 feet tall.

Scarlet Meidiland

Color: Red.

Flower Characteristics: Clusters of heavy blooms. Continuous, all-season bloom. Lightly fragrant.

Plant Characteristics: Dense and spreading. Ideal as ground cover or low hedge in front of fence or wall. Grows 3 to 4 feet tall; produces excellent cut flowers.

Sea Foam

Color: White.

Flower Characteristics: Double, fragrant blooms grow in extraordinary clusters. Lightly fragrant. Abundant bloom with good repeat.

Plant Characteristics: Arching, trailing, and spreading. Grows 3 feet tall and 6 feet wide. Very vigorous and good choice as a ground cover.

White Simplicity

Color: White.

Flower Characteristics: Double blooms grow in clusters. Produces abundant all-season bloom.

Plant Characteristics: Vigorous and disease resistant. Excellent hedge rose if the plants are spaced 18 inches apart. The foliage is bright green and glossy. For a spectacular flower show, plant a border of White Simplicity mixed with either Red or Pink Simplicity. This rose does very well in pots.

Mary Rose

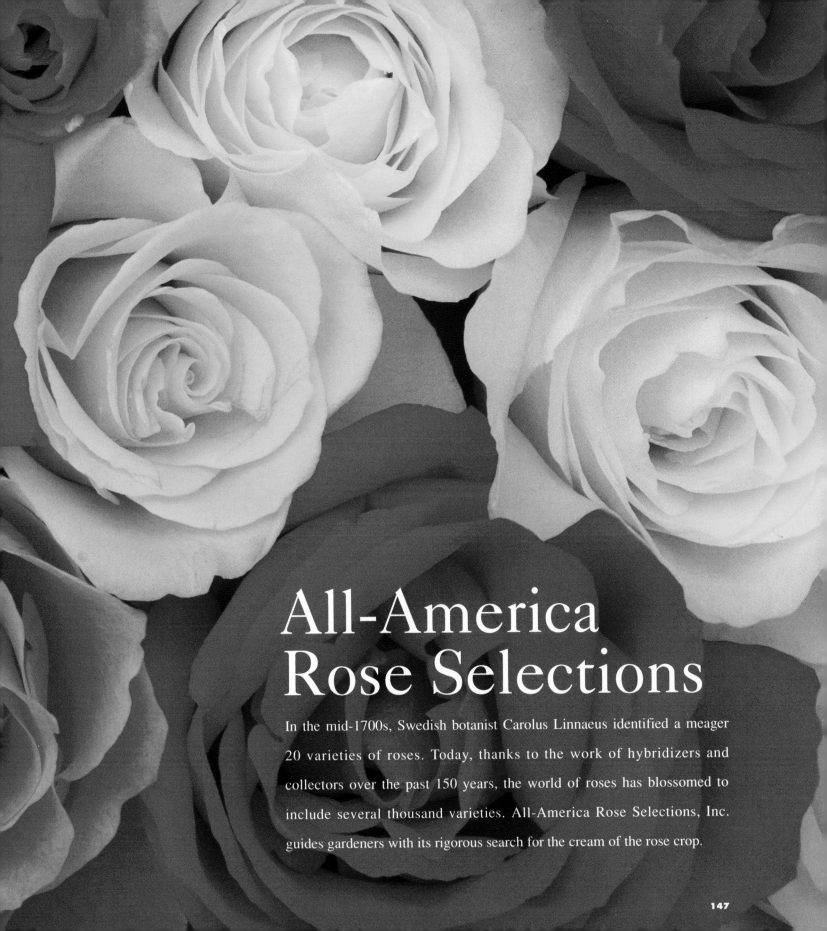

5

All-America Rose Selections

In the mid-1700s, Swedish botanist Carolus Linnaeus identified a meager 20 varieties of roses. Today, thanks to the work of hybridizers and collectors over the past 150 years, the world of roses has blossomed to include several thousand varieties. All-America Rose Selections, Inc. guides gardeners with its rigorous search for the cream of the rose crop.

What Is AARS?

Dedicated to excellence in the rose, All-America Rose Selections, Inc. is a nonprofit association founded in 1938 by a group of rose producers and introducers. Its purpose is to test new rose varieties and recommend only the most exceptional roses to the public.

Under the aegis of AARS, such classic roses as 'Peace,' 'Mister Lincoln,' 'Tropicana,' and 'Queen Elizabeth' have earned the coveted All-America tag, which has become a symbol of strength, beauty, and vitality in roses.

Until the late 1930s, the outlook was anything but rosy for home gardeners hoping to obtain satisfactory rose plants. The rose market in the United States sprouted from a seedling industry after the Civil War and grew unchecked. Thousands of roses were available under a newly enacted plant patent law, yet many were duplicates, marketed under different names, and even more were inferior in quality. There was an urgent need for unbiased research and promotion of roses based on scientific fact.

In 1938, a group of commercial growers headed by such prominent firms as Jackson & Perkins, Armstrong Nurseries, and Conrad-Pyle joined forces with 15 other leading firms to found All-America Rose Selections, Inc. Today, AARS members account for more than 80 percent of the total U.S. rose production.

The first rose trials were held in 1939, and in 1940 the first four All-America Rose Selections winners were named. Since that time, AARS has developed a sophisticated testing program with a nationwide network of test gardens in every region of the country.

The Annual Competition

Of the hundreds of new roses introduced each year, only a handful can hope to survive the rigorous testing process developed by AARS. Spanning the country, the 26 test gardens represent a wide range of climates, and each must maintain standards set by the organization. Roses planted for testing are given the same care that an average home gardener would provide.

Anyone, from professional hybridizer to hobbyist, may enter a new rose variety in the All-America Rose Selections competition, which is open to entrants the world over. By paying an entry fee and supplying test plants to each of the test and demonstration gardens cooperating with AARS, entrants can submit their new rose to a two-year-long scrutiny under the watchful eyes of highly trained AARS judges.

Winning plants must demonstrate exceptional qualities in each of 15 different categories. They also must pass the formidable challenges of Mother Nature, thriving in test gardens from Denver to Disney World, Provo to Portland, Atlanta to Buffalo.

Thousands of roses have competed for the title. As of 1994, only 149 have succeeded, approximately 5 percent of all roses entered since the competition began. The remaining 95 percent have, for the most part, been discarded.

If no rose can run the gauntlet in a given year, AARS declines to name a winner. In its 56-year history, this has happened only once. In 1951 no rose introduction proved equal to the rigid AARS standards. In many years, only one or two winners were selected. AARS bylaws limit the number of winners annually to no more than six.

While not all of the great roses are All-America Rose Selections winners, many favorites are found in this horticultural hall of fame. For the most part, AARS winners have proven worthy and reliable. The majority of garden roses marketed today, in fact, are All-America Rose Selections winners. Such roses as 'Charlotte Armstrong' (1941), 'Tiffany' (1955), 'First Prize' (1970), 'Double Delight' (1977), 'Honor' (1980), 'French Lace' (1982), and many others have won the hearts of rose devotees everywhere.

Entering its second half-century, All-America Rose Selections has proven a valuable yardstick for measuring the quality of America's favorite flower.

Shining Hour, 1991 Award Winner

Sweet Inspiration, 1993 Award Winner

Creating a New Rose

To enter All-America Rose Selections competition, a rose must be a new specimen, a hybrid. Whether produced by an amateur or a professional, rose hybrids are the creative offspring of science and artistry.

Rose hybridizing began in France during the reign of Empress Josephine to enhance her famous rose garden at Malmaison. With advances in technique and knowledge, hybridizers have developed the magnificent quality and variety of roses available today.

While the term "hybrid" is familiar, the actual process by which a new rose is developed is a mystery to most amateurs.

The first step in hybridizing a rose is taking pollen from the male portion of one rose, the stamen, and applying it to the pistil, or female organ, of a different variety. If fertilization succeeds, a "hip" or seed capsule grows and four to six seeds will develop. If they germinate, a new rose is born.

Once a cross is produced, the young flower is tagged with the names of its parents, then covered with plastic to prevent insects or weather from interfering with the pollination process.

The seeds are harvested in late summer or fall and planted in a greenhouse. The following spring, when they are large enough, the young seedlings are transplanted outdoors.

As the plants develop and blossom, the rose hybridizer analyzes their characteristics, rejecting all but a select group of the finest. The odds against a new specimen are tremendous. As few as two per 10,000 seedlings may be allowed to continue for further study and testing.

If a new rose demonstrates the strength, character, and charm that are prerequisites for entry in the All-America Rose Selections competition, it is then entered into trials for further observation and scoring by AARS judges over two years. To become an All-America Rose Selections winner, the newcomer must be truly a breed apart.

Solitude, 1993 Award Winner

Test Garden Program

Spanning the country, a group of carefully selected and monitored gardens serve as the testing grounds for the AARS program. Here, fledgling roses try their wings in real garden settings in diverse climates. While professionally managed and maintained, these gardens do not pamper their charges. A rose receives the care it might hope for in an average home garden.

The 26 gardens include the many different climate and soil conditions found in the regions in which roses are cultivated. In the mild coastal conditions of southern California, in the subtropical warmth of Florida, under damp Pacific Northwest skies, and in frigid Midwest and Northeast conditions, each rose must prove worthy or it is weeded out by the testing process.

An official AARS judge is

assigned to serve at each garden. Chosen for their experience and horticultural expertise, these men and women often are curators of well-known rose gardens or are university professors.

Originally, all AARS test gardens were located on the grounds of the member firms. Over the years, however, AARS has shifted the test sites to locations at universities or large public gardens. All official AARS test gardens are now, as a matter of policy, nonmember operations. Although AARS member firms, who are engaged in the business of growing and selling roses, were never criticized for operating the test gardens in earlier years, the organization decided it would be best to turn this function over to nonmembers.

The goal of the test program, according to the AARS Judges Guidebook, is "to foster the development, production, and

distribution of new and better roses in and for the United States of America."

While the research program has successfully met that goal for more than 50 years, another benefit to the public is the opportunity to view the new roses in a garden setting firsthand. By visiting an AARS garden in bloom, home gardeners can pass their own judgment on a new rose rather than purchase it sight unseen. In these beautiful surroundings, the visitor can stroll through drifts of color and fragrance and keep a private scorecard. How do you rate the latest All-America Rose contestants? There's nothing like seeing, sniffing, and judging for yourself.

Public Rose Gardens

In addition to the test gardens, AARS. has named 139 official accredited public rose gardens nationwide. These gardens, located in 43 states and the District of Columbia, serve as showcases for AARS award winners and offer a glimpse of a spectacular summer show staged by roses en masse. Displayed in beds with plants numbering in the thousands, beautifully tended roses of every hue form a floral tapestry of breathtaking color and fragrance. From the grounds of the United Nations in New York City to Walt Disney World in Orlando, Florida, from historic Longwood Gardens in Pennsylvania's Kennett Square, to Tyler, Texas, which boasts one of the nation's largest rose gardens, the AARS public gardens are enjoyed by millions annually.

Local rose societies often help maintain the gardens. To retain their accreditation, the gardens must comply with standards set by the AARS Public Gardens Committee. A garden's appearance and care, use by the public, and efforts to provide information and other services to the public are all evaluated annually. As a result, most Americans do not have to travel far to preview each year's new All-America award winners and enjoy older varieties as well. See page 216 for a list of AARS test gardens and public rose gardens.

Class Act, 1989 Award Winner

6

The New Look of Old Roses

Imagine the "perfect" rose: one that combines the beauty and fragrance of old garden roses with the hardy, easy-care traits of modern roses. In recent years, matchmaking hybridizers in England and France have successfully married the two. Their offspring are two new breeds of roses that blend the best characteristics of their ancestors.

English Roses

Although hybrid teas and floribundas have dominated rose gardens over the past few decades, the romance of old roses has lingered. The roses that graced the gardens of our great-grandparents continue to have a small but devoted cadre of followers. Once intoxicated by their delicious fragrances, full-bodied form, and lovely shades of pink, mauve, and carmine, few can resist the charm of antique roses.

The antique varieties are not without their flaws, however. Most old roses bloom only once at the beginning of the season and repeat weakly, if at all. Their rosy colors can seem monotonous to gardeners who long for the spicy hues available in hybrid teas.

For American rose fanciers, it's now possible to have the best of both worlds. Considered by many authorities to be the greatest advance in rose breeding in the past 50 years, a new breed of shrub roses combines the classic virtues of old roses with the colors and other sterling qualities of modern roses. Available in Great Britain for almost three decades, the English roses of David Austin are relative newcomers to the United States.

The Englishman responsible for this revolution comes from a farming family in Shropshire. Turning his hand to nursery work, Austin devoted himself to growing old-fashioned roses. Not content to grow what was already on the market, he decided to breed his own strain. An expert in antique varieties, Austin at age 21 envisioned developing a new type of rose that would preserve the many virtues of classic roses while eliminating their weaknesses.

It took Austin 12 years and thousands of attempts before he introduced his first rose. A cross between 'Dainty Maid,' a pink floribunda from 1940, and 'Belle Isis,' a pink gallica dating to 1845, Austin created a hardy new rose with huge pink, cup-shape flowers. Named 'Constance Spry,' it created a stir in England and gave the world its first glimpse of a new type of rose. Austin crossed the rose with other floribundas, continuing his quest for a more perfect rose.

After 40 years of labor in hybridizing antique and modern roses, Austin has developed a collection of more than 90 new roses. Modestly, he calls his creations simply "English roses," but they also are known as a group as the David Austin roses.

Available in a rich palette of colors, heights, and types of flowers, the roses are gaining more attention with every season. Their pleasing blend of old-fashioned fragrance and form with modern disease resistance and repeat bloom characteristics recommend them for mixed borders, hedges, and traditional rose beds.

Like old roses, the English roses lean toward pastel colors, but also offer some luscious "modern" yellows, apricots, and blends. Their flowers retain the voluptuous cabbage forms—double and semidouble rosettes of many petals, cup-and-saucer shapes, and single whorls of five petals. Their fragrances pay homage to the roses of yesteryear, too. Ranging from rich to intense, their perfume marks their antique lineage as strongly as their form and color.

Gardeners who have tested David Austin roses in the United States and Canada have found them to be reliable performers in North American soils and climates. They do require extra winter protection in harsher regions, particularly through their first season, however.

You may be so smitten by these roses that you'll want to try them all. If you have room for just one, consider 'Gertrude Jekyll.' Named for the English garden designer, this shrub rose offers a sumptuous soft pink flower in a classic old rose form. The blossoms come in waves all summer long, and the shrub develops healthy, disease-resistant growth that makes it a lovely addition to a perennial border.

David Austin calls his cultivars "new roses in the old tradition." Each plant is an original, yet even the names reflect their proud English parentage. Many of the new roses bear the names of characters from

Chaucer and Shakespeare, such as 'Prospero,' 'The Squire,' 'The Wife of Bath,' and 'Othello.' Names for other favorites were borrowed from family members—'Lillian Austin,' 'Charles Austin,' and 'Francis Austin.'

The colors of English roses roam the palette. 'Abraham Darby' has a lush apricot and whorled petal pattern. 'Emanuel' combines pink, salmon, and lemon with a quartered and flat blossom. 'Lillian Austin' opens from copper orange buds to salmon mousse flowers. Deep garnet marks the large double flowers of 'Fisherman's Friend,' which also has a powerful fragrance. 'Othello' is another dusky crimson flower, which fades to purple and mauve. 'L. D. Braithwaite' is the deepest red in an enormous saucer-size blossom. 'William Shakespeare,' like one of its parents, 'The Squire,' is a deep crimson with gallicalike blooms.

White Austin roses tend to creamy buffs. An example is 'English Garden,' which has exquisite buttery flowers. A 3-foot-high plant, it has a light, fresh fragrance. Other white beauties include 'Francis Austin' and 'Saint Cecilia.' Pinks are well represented with 'The Countryman,' a bright rose-pink; 'Sir Walter Raleigh,' a large pink flower showing golden stamens; 'Warwick Castle,' a headily scented double of deep pink; and 'Heritage,' with fragrant and profuse blush pink blossoms.

Yellows are crowned by 'Graham Thomas,' with its rich golden flowers. 'Windrush' opens from butter gold buds into chalky yellow flowers. 'Swan' is yellow fading to white, and 'Symphony' has a beautiful yellow rosette, creamy at the edges.

Like their forebears, English roses are more shrublike than the typical hybrid tea. Their handsome foliage and arching loose form give them remarkable flexibility in the landscape.

Heralded by some as the finest yellow rose of all time, 'Graham Thomas' *(far left)* was named for a renowned English rose expert. Its golden yellow petals develop from apricot pink buds.

'Othello' *(above)* takes center stage clad in velvety, deep crimson petals that slowly age to purple and mauve. Richly fragrant, its oversize blossoms perform well in the garden and in mixed bouquets.

As delicate as a cup of fine English porcelain, 'Fair Bianca' *(left)* has china white blossoms that open from round buds into the classic flattened shape of an antique rose.

Landscape Roses

The Meidiland Roses of France

If low-maintenance rose gardening is your aim, consider a feisty new breed of French imports. The House of Meilland offers roses that combine spectacular beauty and minimal maintenance.

Practically self-sufficient, these scrappy shrub roses are disease-resistant, ever-blooming hybrids. Yet they're as pretty as they are practical. Handsome foliage makes a rich green frame for spectacular blossoms that continue all summer.

A new concept in roses, these shrubs were bred by the House of Meilland, French rose hybridizers who gave the world many of the loveliest roses of the 20th century. Like their cousins, the David Austin roses from across the English Channel, the Meidiland family of landscape roses is rapidly colonizing gardens on this side of the Atlantic.

The Meidilands are a hardy, carefree strain, ideal for gardeners who haven't the time or patience to deal with finicky plants. These versatile shrub roses are easy-care and easy to grow, unlike the often-demanding hybrid teas and floribundas that dominate most rose gardens. With little or no pruning, the Meidilands will prosper year in and year out. A light tip pruning in spring with hedge shears is the most some will require. The Meidilands also are disease resistant and need little spraying.

Best of all, the Meidiland roses are hardy anywhere in the contiguous United States. Because they grow on their own roots, these roses will come back true-to-name, even if winter kills them back to the ground.

Some varieties add bonus off-season color to the garden with bright red fruits and brilliantly colored canes. Meidiland roses are ideal as shrubs, hedges, ground covers, and specimens.

Five varieties of Meidiland roses are available in the United States through catalogs and nurseries. They are recommended for planting in zones 3–10. The color spectrum includes white, pink, and red, and they span a range of heights, from 2 to 5 feet. Vigorous and fast growing, Meidilands are ideal for use as rapid-spreading ground cover and hedges, adding mass color to the landscape quickly.

Bonica

The first and only shrub rose to win the coveted All-America Rose Selections award, 'Bonica' keeps on flowering. Soft pink, very double flowers in clusters of 20 or more cover the deep green glossy foliage all summer long. This 4-foot-high plant will give you enough bouquets to fill every room.

'Bonica' can be pruned to form a hedge or low screen or left to spread naturally to its full 5-foot width. It needs only light tip pruning for routine care. Even at rest in fall and winter, 'Bonica' adds color to the garden with bright red rose hips dangling from its branches like Christmas tree ornaments.

Scarlet Meidiland

A steep slope or rock wall is the preferred spot for 'Scarlet Meidiland.' Only 3 feet tall when full-grown, this mounding ground cover will spread 5 to 6 feet, but rarely needs pruning. It takes more shade than most other roses. Brilliant crimson flowers begin in June and repeat all summer and fall. The blooms are exceptionally long lasting, lingering unfaded for up to two weeks. In bouquets, cut flowers will last up to a week. The foliage is small and deep green.

Pink Meidiland

'Pink Meidiland' (right) makes a prize specimen in a Victorian or cottage-style garden. Planted in groups, it forms a cloud of fragrant color. Its shell pink single flowers are long lasting and bloom continuously, spring into fall.

Soft-green leaves are lightly glossy. The plant grows to 4 feet tall and will spread to 3½ feet wide. In the

fall the shrub develops orange-red hips that linger well into winter. This worry-free rose has a vigorous constitution and requires only a light tip pruning in the spring.

White Meidiland

If you're weary of lawn mowing, 'White Meidiland' (left) is the perfect alternative for sunny spots. Growing 2 feet high, each plant will spread 4 to 5 feet. The pure white double flowers smother the plant in blossoms. Borne profusely in clusters, the flowers start in June, repeating all summer and fall. The dark forest green leaves are large and glossy, hiding the canes completely.

A perfect ground cover, this rose requires no pruning, but deadheading will help prolong the beauty of the blossoms.

Sevillana

Another scarlet lady, this rose makes a dazzling hedge or mass planting, or shines all alone in the garden. Deep crimson flowers open in dense clusters, with a nonstop, four-month show. Red hips replace the blossoms, decorating, the branches for winter.

Eventually reaching 4 feet tall with a 3-foot spread, 'Sevillana' is another of the Meidiland pest- and disease-resistant rose garden workhorses.

7

Rose Garden Design

Pretty rose gardens are not just a matter of beautiful plants, hard work, and a little luck. It takes a solid design to turn an assortment of fine plants into a garden showplace. Tradition and fashion suggest many possible designs, from formal to frivolous, but the best gardens are personal, suited to the gardener and the yard.

In a well-designed garden, the beds, borders, paths, and garden structures are accessible and inviting. Careful planning also takes the horticultural needs of roses into account, which makes the garden easier to maintain. In the absence of a plan, a garden may consist of a few almost incidentally placed spots of charm. Good design unifies the whole garden and establishes its personality.

Choosing a Style

Like a magnificent landscape painting, the garden should draw the eye and the strolling gardener through a foreground, a middle depth, and into the background. These layers may be created by roses alone, or by roses in pleasing combinations with other plants and garden furnishings.

Whether the garden is carefully structured or naturalistic, the yard's size and shape and the location of the house should influence, and may suggest, the basic design.

Balance and proportion and unity and repetition are fundamental design elements. These become the bones of the garden—the skeleton of the plan—which is filled out with plants.

Taking advantage of a good view and screening a less desirable one often are important concerns. Place the garden where you can best enjoy it. A rose garden around a patio brings color and fragrance up close; a rose garden in the yard makes an attractive destination. The color and fragrance of roses along a garden path is always welcoming.

Traditional all-rose gardens are the most formal. They usually are based on a neat geometric arrangement of beds and tidy intersecting paths, often of well-laid brick or stone. High walls, trimmed hedges, and arbors provide definition and substance. Well-ordered and well-kept formal gardens are both refreshing and soothing. These gardens usually are showplaces for long-stem hybrid tea roses, but a modern interpretation could include many different roses, from rugosas to miniatures.

Informal rose gardens use natural shapes and groupings of plants.

Right angles give way to casual curves, and balance and variety replace strict symmetry. The roses are focal points against colorful drifts of other flowers and masses of textured greenery. The informal rose garden is likely to be framed by a line of trees, a mixed border of shrubs, or a fine old fence or wall, and paths may seem to drift lazily through the garden. Here the fragrance of roses may blend with the scent of pungent herbs, and native plants may share space with the latest hybrid introductions.

What Roses Need

For a healthy, vigorous rose garden, choose a site with care, and take the time and trouble to improve the soil before planting.

Roses need at least five hours of full sun a day; most professionals recommend six as the absolute minimum. Without enough sun, rose bushes become spindly and bloom only sparingly. If you have a choice, southern exposure provides the best light. An eastern exposure with morning sun also is desirable; it dries the dew from foliage early in the day, which helps control fungal diseases. A western exposure can be very strong in the afternoon heat, and light shade is acceptable. Low-light northern exposures are the least desirable.

Good air circulation is crucial to keep fungal diseases to a minimum, but the garden should have some shelter from high winds and harsh weather. Wind steals moisture from the soil, and temperature swings in an exposed garden put stress on rose bushes. It is best not to plant too close to trees, which compete aggressively with roses for moisture and nutrients in the soil.

Flat ground is easier to work with than a sloping area, but a curved, descending walk, with terraces to control the grade, makes a graceful rose garden on a hill.

The soil should drain well. Roses are long-lived plants with roots

In this formal garden, mature trees and elegant architecture around the property frame a traditional all-rose garden, with boxwood hedges as the only accent.

that extend deep into the ground. If the soil holds water for too long, the roots will rot. Check the drainage by digging a hole large enough to hold about a gallon of water. Fill it, and if water stands in the hole, you should improve the drainage.

Adding organic material such as leaf mold, compost, or peat moss will improve the soil dramatically; a healthy organic content encourages good drainage in tightly compacted soil and helps retain moisture in sandy soil. Organic material also improves the soil structure and adds nutrients. A compost heap will provide a steady supply of rich humus to work into the soil and to use as mulch.

Where poor drainage is a real problem, raise the planting area with low brick or stone walls, or with landscaping timbers. This lifts the roses a little above the saturated soil.

Work the soil with a garden fork or rototiller, turning in compost, dehydrated cow manure, peat moss, and other amendments. Dig 2 feet deep if possible, but at least 18 inches. The prepared soil should be well mixed, crumbly, and free of large stones.

Gardening on Paper

Once you have an idea of the style of garden you would like and an understanding of what roses need, the design process can begin. It is a good idea to make a map of your garden, using plain graph paper. The house's title plot may provide the basic outline, but check all the measurements at the start. Draw in property lines; the house; walks and driveway; patio, porch, or deck; and permanent structures. Sketch in existing landscaping, especially mature trees. Allow for the canopy of the trees, including trees in neighboring yards. Date your map.

Walk around the property, observing light and shadows and the lay of the land. Consider the traffic patterns of your family and pets. Then let your yard and its character help suggest the rose garden's design. Use the property lines to advantage, but resist following them too strictly. Island gardens, or flower beds that fill in a sunny corner, add new angles to the property's basic shape.

Look at the yard from inside the house, too. For most gardeners, decorating tastes, the architecture of the house, and the rose garden will all fit together.

Sketch your plans for the rose garden on separate sheets of paper, and plot the ones you like best on the map. Go ahead and try a number of ideas on paper, while a pencil is the only tool you will need to work with. There will be plenty of time for digging later. Be realistic about how large a garden you can take care of.

Once you have a design, mark off the new garden in the yard, using stakes and string, or, for curved lines, a garden hose. Walk around and through the plan, looking at the spaces from all angles. Are the paths wide enough? Is there enough room for a bench or an arbor? Some central feature—a fountain, birdbath, reflecting ball, or other ornament—usually is an appealing addition. If the garden has a gate, an arbor for climbing roses is a natural choice, but make it tall enough so garden guests will not have to duck, and wide enough for wheelbarrows and other equipment.

Professional Plans

There are no absolute rules in garden design, only guidelines. Professionals look at both space and volume to design a garden that is well proportioned, both horizontally and vertically, no matter what its size or style. Look for ideas in books and magazines, and visit public and private gardens. Borrow ideas freely, adapting them to your own garden design.

The garden should be in scale with the house and yard. The garden should function well on the human scale, too. Use yourself as a standard measure, and design the garden so its pleasing to you. Trust your instincts, but try to train your eye. Narrow paths leave plenty of room for roses, but a more substantial and well-defined path will lead the eye and direct the feet, and give substance to the plan. Generous proportions in scale with the house, site, and roses are attractive and welcoming.

A strong background helps establish the rose garden's place in

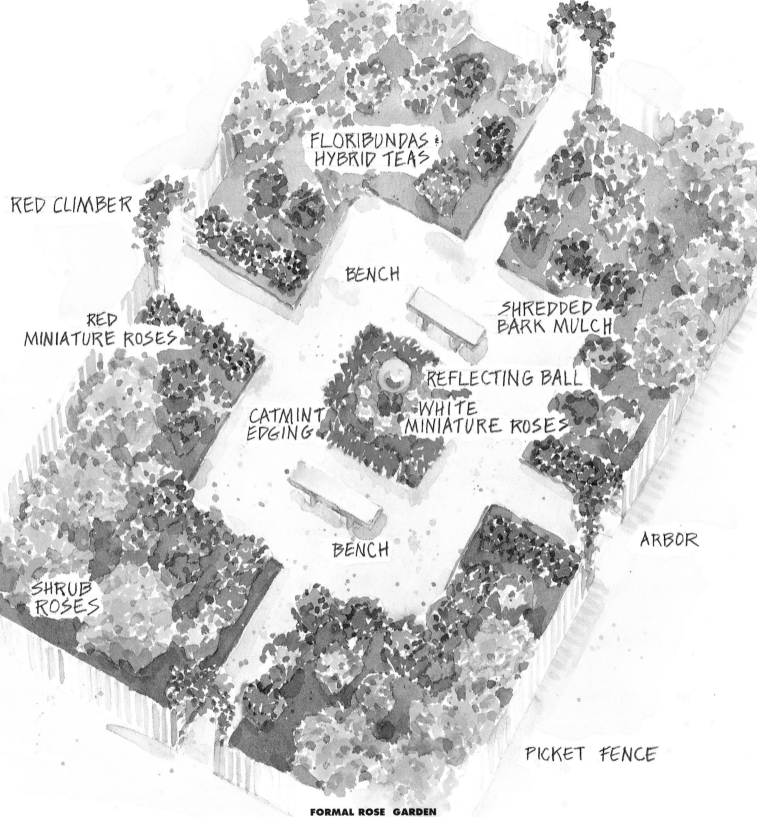

RED CLIMBER

FLORIBUNDAS &
HYBRID TEAS

BENCH

SHREDDED
BARK MULCH

RED
MINIATURE ROSES

REFLECTING BALL

CATMINT
EDGING

WHITE
MINIATURE ROSES

BENCH

ARBOR

SHRUB
ROSES

PICKET FENCE

FORMAL ROSE GARDEN
Roses of all types grow within the geometric beds of this classic formal rose garden.

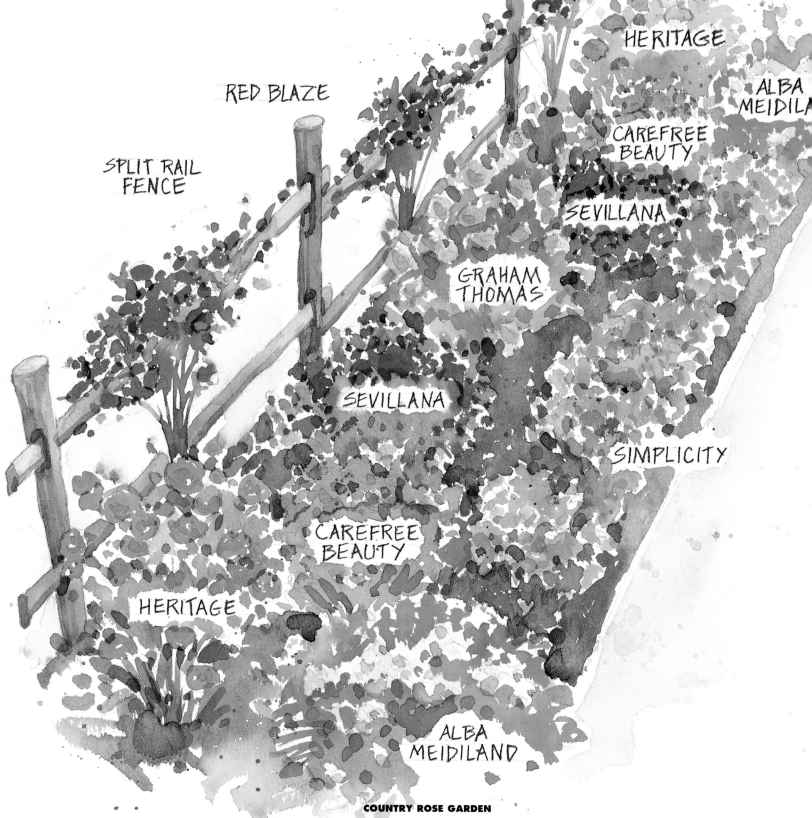

HERITAGE

ALBA MEIDILA

RED BLAZE

CAREFREE BEAUTY

SPLIT RAIL FENCE

SEVILLANA

GRAHAM THOMAS

SEVILLANA

SIMPLICITY

CAREFREE BEAUTY

HERITAGE

ALBA MEIDILAND

COUNTRY ROSE GARDEN

In the country garden, bright clusters of perennials keep the garden colorful while the roses go in and out of bloom.

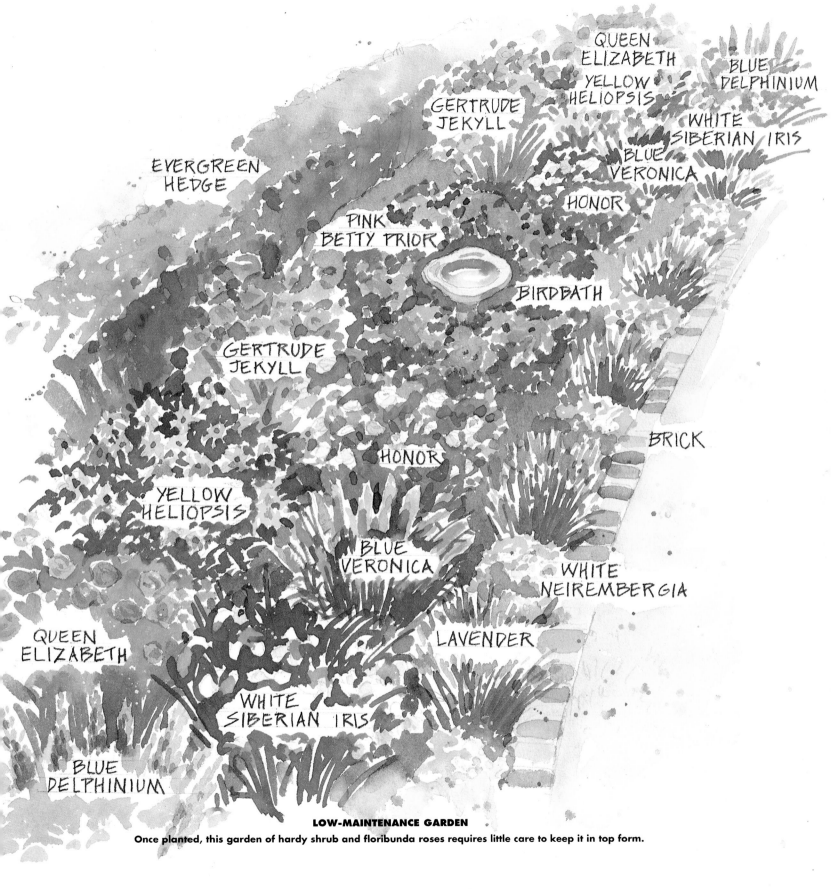

LOW-MAINTENANCE GARDEN
Once planted, this garden of hardy shrub and floribunda roses requires little care to keep it in top form.

177

the landscaping. The formal garden design on page 175 has both a fence around it and tall shrub roses as a backdrop for the hybrid tea and floribunda roses planted beside the paths. The overlapping colors and textures of the plants add rhythm to the design. Pay careful attention to details: In the formal garden, white miniature roses just inside a border of catmint form part of the centerpiece; red miniature roses at the garden's main gates mark the path like footlights.

Work with the color and texture of both flowers and foliage. Plants that provide interest through several seasons will make the garden a source of pleasure year-round. In the mixed border shown in the country garden on page 176, the classic grandiflora rose 'Queen Elizabeth' is planted near 'Gertrude Jekyll,' a David Austin rose. Bright heliopsis between them and free-flowering, creamy siberian iris in front complement the pink roses. Clumps of blue sage and a border of lavender interplanted with white annual nierembergia in complementary hues add variety, texture, and fragrance.

Variety and balance should be part of every design. In the plan for a low-maintenance garden on page 177, three vigorous 'Blaze' roses clamber along a split-rail fence to form a backdrop. 'Sevilliana' and 'Carefree Beauty' roses, flanked by 'Heritage' roses, establish a red and pink color scheme. The yellow rose 'Graham Thomas' is used as a sunny centerpiece. 'Simplicity' roses make a low hedge in front, and 'White Meidiland' roses anchor the corners. There is variety among the rose bushes but balance and unity in the design.

Architectural elements contribute significantly to a garden's design and deserve special attention from the start. Garden seats and shelters should be sturdy, comfortable, and near enough to plantings that you can smell the roses. If roses are planted in containers, the pots or boxes should be large enough for the roses, sturdy enough to withstand wind and weather, and compatible in style with the garden and its setting.

Whether they are straight or curved, the garden's beds should be clearly defined. The edges may blur in summer's exuberant growth, but it should be clear where the garden stops and the yard begins. The simplest edge is a crisp break in the lawn, maintained with a sharp spade, but bricks, stone, or a border of liriope, for example, all work well in a rose garden. Natural material almost always looks better than plastic. Pathways can be paved with brick or stone, wood planks, wood rounds or blocks, chipped bark, gravel, or loose fill, which is a mixture of pebbles, crushed rock, sand, shredded bark, nutshells, seashells, and pine straw.

Give yourself and the roses plenty of room. Plants will develop and change as they mature, and so will your tastes, so resist the temptation to plant too close together at the start. Spaces can be filled in with annual flowers until roses and other plants reach their full size. A good design will look as though nature had a hand in it.

Roses for Every Garden

The key to success in selecting and growing roses is to choose carefully. Do not go to the nursery on a bright Saturday morning in May and fall in love with 20 roses. Do your research on the cultural needs of roses you like, then pick those that fit your garden's plan and your own style.

When selecting roses, first look for those that perform well in your climate. Spare yourself the frustration of planting tender roses where winters are brutal. Cold-hardiness zone ratings should be your guide, but make a note of roses that thrive in public and private gardens where you live.

Pick roses not only for their flower color and fragrance, but also for the size and shape of the bush and the color and texture of the foliage. There is surprising variety in the foliage of roses, from deep

This relatively new half-moon garden has a classic appeal in its commitment to symmetry. Potted plants link the garden and the deck, and the trellis frames the view of the garden.

green to apple green leaves. Some have interesting fall color, or bright red or orange hips that linger into the winter months.

Each rose has its own personality. Some are thorny and independent, others tame. Sizes range from neat miniatures to substantial old roses that send canes arching as much as 15 feet every year. Use rugosas and old roses to fill large gaps in the landscaping. Place tall plants toward the back of a bed or border, or use them as centerpieces, with more compact roses in front. Plant floribundas and hybrid tea roses in groups for clouds of color in the garden.

Combining Roses

All roses go together, but some combinations work better than others. Roses with flowers of the same color, but differing in shades and intensities, will have a bold effect. The size and shape of the plants, their growth habits, and the style of the garden will influence your choices.

Green is the universal color in the garden and mixes well with any color. Pink, yellow, and red combine naturally, and most roses fall within this range. White roses go with everything.

Place tall roses at the back of a border, or in the center of a bed. Climbing roses are best in the background or on a fence or wall. Leave the smallest roses in the front. Roses in containers can be used as accents.

Here are some possible combinations:

• Red roses: Everyone loves red roses. Plant 'Chrysler Imperial' with 'Double Delight' and 'Mr. Lincoln.' An arbor planted with 'Don Juan' and 'Dr. Huey' shows off a mix of flower forms in luxurious, deep red.

• Roses with bright hips or distinctive fall foliage: The rugosa roses 'Delicata,' 'Fru Dagmar Hastrup,' and 'Blanc Double de Coubert' look pretty even in winter. Shrub roses 'Betty Prior,' 'Carefree Wonder,' and 'Simplicity' bloom well into fall, as does 'Aloha,' a climbing hybrid tea.

• Pinks: There are many beautiful pink roses in every class. A few favorites are 'Bonica,' 'The Fairy,' 'Mme. Isaac Pereire,' 'Sonia,' 'Chicago Peace,' 'Sarah Van Fleet,' and 'Cupcake.'

• Apricot and orange: Pair the climber 'Alchymist' with 'Cornelia' or 'Lady Penzance' to form a backdrop for 'Gruss an Aachen,' 'Just Joey,' or 'Whisky Mac.' These roses have rich coppery tones that combine well with soft pinks.

• White or cream: Use these roses to accent rich rose colors: 'Iceberg,' 'Boule de Neige,' 'Fair Bianca,' 'Honor,' 'Alba,' 'Little White Pet,' and 'Margaret Merrill.'

In this country garden, roses overtake a lattice shelter. Bright clusters of perennials provide contrast, from the strappy leaves of iris to feathery daisies and coreopsis.

8

Care and Maintenance

Selecting your favorite roses is only the beginning of your flower-filled

dreams of cultivating a rose garden. There's soil preparation to tend to first,

then planting, pruning, feeding, watering, and pest and disease control.

With tender care from the start, your rose garden will repay you with fresh

bouquets of blooms every spring, summer, and fall.

Planting Roses

Planting time officially arrives when garden centers begin stocking their racks with bare-root roses. Available only early in the growing season, these harbingers of spring should be planted when they're dormant and the ground is not frozen. In warm regions, the best time is late winter. Where temperatures never drop below zero degrees Fahrenheit, planting may be done in early spring or late fall. In areas of extreme cold, bare-root roses should be planted only in the spring.

If the bare-root season has come and gone, you can purchase potted roses, already leafed out and growing. Available at local nurseries throughout the gardening season, potted roses can be planted any time during warm weather, allowing you to fill bare spots in your garden where color is needed most.

Proper Placement

Whether you prefer starting with bare-root or potted roses, make sure that you place the roses properly in your yard. Plant roses where they will receive at least six hours of direct sunlight each day. (Miniature and climbing roses are able to tolerate a little more shade than their larger cousins and are happy to bask in the dappled shade from an ornamental tree.)

If you have the choice of morning or afternoon sun, morning sun is best because it quickly dries the dew on plant foliage, decreasing the risk of disease. Where summers are intensely hot and dry, give roses some relief from the high temperatures and glare by placing them in a location that gets light afternoon shade. To shield delicate blooms from damaging winds, choose a protected garden location, near a fence, hedge, or structure.

Place roses where they can stay put and will not have to be moved in two or three years. Don't plant roses where their roots will compete with roots from other trees and shrubs. If this is impossible, install underground barriers made from impenetrable and durable material, such as aluminum siding. Place it so that the competing roots will stay away from the roses yet give the rose roots room to grow.

Spacing Roses

The amount of space you allow between bushes depends on your climate and the type of rose you're planting. Because roses require good air circulation to discourage insects and fungus diseases, it's

Exotically colored blooms on the hybrid tea 'Rio Samba' turn from yellow in the centers to orange on the petal edges.

To plant a potted rose, dig a hole slightly larger and deeper than the container. Slit the side of the pot with a sharp knife and carefully remove the rose without disturbing the root ball. Position the rose in the hole at the proper level, where the bud union (the knob at the base of the canes) aligns with the ground. Fill in around the root ball with soil, gently firming it with your hands. Water thoroughly.

Old-fashioned climbers 'Evangeline' and 'Felicite Parmentier,' smother this arbor with summer blooms.

Mail-order nurseries often offer a wider selection of varieties than neighborhood outlets. If you purchase roses through a catalog, bare-root plants will be sent to you at the time they can be safely planted in your area.

When you receive your shipment, open the box immediately and inspect the plants. The canes should be green and plump, and the roots pliable and damp. Shriveled or broken canes and roots indicate that the plants have been damaged or allowed to dry out during their transport.

Bare-root roses should be planted as soon as possible after they arrive. If, for some reason, planting must be postponed, keep the roots moist by misting them with water and wrapping each bush—including the canes—in dampened newspaper. Place the plants in a large plastic bag and store for up to two weeks in a cool, dark place. Check the roots every day or two and dampen the newspaper when necessary. For longer delays, heel plants in the ground by digging a 1-foot-deep trench in a cool, shaded spot; loosely cover the roots and canes with soil.

Planting Preparations

Before planting bare-root roses, cut off any broken or damaged roots and canes with pruning shears. Soak the roots in a bucket of tepid water overnight (or for as long as 24 hours) to restore moisture to the canes lost during shipping. Because roots dry out quickly, keep them in the water until the moment you set them in the garden.

Planting instructions for bare-root roses are outlined in the illustrations on the opposite page.

After your roses are in place, remove the variety label, usually a metal tag attached to a cane with wire. (The wire might eventually injure the cane or be inadvertently discarded during pruning.) Attach the label to a stake and place it in the ground near the bush. Keep a separate record of the varieties you plant and their location in the garden.

important to avoid crowding them. In most regions of the country, hybrid teas, grandifloras, and floribundas should be planted 24 inches apart. Where winters are mild and growing seasons are longer, space roses farther apart—about 3 feet—to allow for bigger bush sizes. Plant the larger shrub roses and old garden roses at least 4 to 6 feet apart, depending on their mature size.

For climbers to be trained horizontally along a fence, allow a distance of 8 to 10 feet between plants. Miniature roses can be spaced as close as 12 inches apart in cold climates, 18 inches apart in warm areas.

Most roses are sold in bare-root form. Harvested from growers' fields when they're dormant, the plants are shipped to local retailers and mail-order buyers with protective wrapping around their roots.

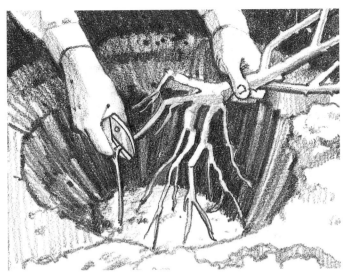

Dig a hole 24 inches deep and wide. Mound the soil at the bottom of the hole. Set the plant on top of the mound, spreading out the roots on all sides. Position the bud union so that it is aligned with ground level.

Backfill the hole two-thirds full, firming the soil with your hands. Add water, and allow it to drain. Fill the hole to the top with soil; mound additional soil around canes. Make a well around the mound for water.

Prune canes back by a third after planting, and remove any dead or broken wood. This will direct the plant's energy to the growth of new, strong canes from the start. Water plants often until they're established.

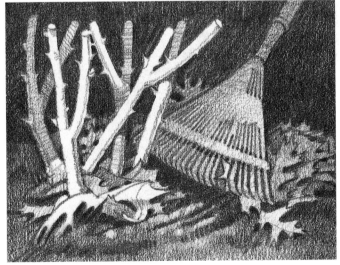

Protect canes from chilly, drying winds with an organic mulch, such as leaves or shredded bark. Keep the mulch in place until new growth shows on canes, then remove it with a leaf rake or your hands.

Pruning Roses

An annual pruning regimen helps keep roses healthy and blooming. Newly planted roses require little pruning the first few years, except for the removal of weak, dead, or diseased wood. In following years, however, pruning is necessary to control the size and shape of plants.

Prune established roses when the buds begin to swell, sometime between midwinter and midspring, depending on your climate. If forsythias grow in the area, their yellow blooms signal the time to prune roses. Prune first to remove dead wood. Cut these canes flush with the bud union. Never leave stumps; they become entry points for insects and diseases. Next, prune damaged or diseased wood, cutting below the injury or discolored area to the white pith. Then, clip off weak, spindly branches. To improve air circulation, remove canes that are growing into the center of the plant, and those that crisscross. Make cuts at a 45-degree angle about ¼ inch above a bud. Prune to a bud that faces out, to keep the plant open.

Such pruning should leave healthy canes; remove all but three or four of the strongest and youngest. How much you prune the remaining canes depends on the rose type. In cold climates, winterkill may determine the pruning height. Prune hybrid teas and floribundas to a height of 12 to 18 inches. (If floribundas are used as a hedge, prune plants higher, and leave more canes for dense growth.) Leave grandifloras taller, 18 to 24 inches high.

Long-stemmed pink-and-yellow blooms on 'Broadway' hybrid tea rose win rave reviews for the beauty they bring to bouquets.

On hybrid teas, remove dead wood first, cutting canes flush with the bud union. Next, prune diseased or broken branches to the point where the pith is white. Make these cuts at a 45-degree angle about ¼ inch above an outside-facing bud.

To improve air circulation, remove weak, spindly branches, and canes that grow into the center of the plant. Select three or four of the newest and strongest canes to remain on the plant, and remove all others flush with the bud union.

Trim tree roses to keep branches evenly spaced and symmetrical. Prune miniatures to about half their summer height. Timing is critical when pruning climbing roses. Because most climbers bloom on old wood, you'll cut away the flower show if you prune too early. Avoid pruning climbing roses in the spring, except to trim dead wood. Put climbers on your list of summer chores.

Hybrid perpetuals also bloom from the previous season's growth. Though you can prune them in spring, be sure to preserve the year-old growth, and remove only the oldest canes. The same advice applies to shrub and old garden roses; limit removal to old, weak, or dead wood, then shape the remaining branches, leaving them tall and natural. Like shrub roses, polyanthas are hardy and seldom suffer from winter dieback; cut canes back by half their former height, and remove the oldest canes.

Pruning Tools

One of the best investments you can make is proper pruning tools. For best results, use curved-edge pruning shears. Avoid straight-edge anvil types, which can crush canes as they cut. For thick branches on old garden roses, shrub roses, and climbers, use long-handled loppers or a pruning saw.

To ensure clean, healthy cuts, sharpen your pruning tools regularly; jagged wounds left by dull shears heal slowly, making the plant more vulnerable to insects and diseases. Dip tools in disinfectant after each use to prevent the spread of disease from plant to plant.

Each time you prune, discard all cuttings, which may harbor pests and disease spores. Seal pruning cuts on branches that are ½ inch in diameter or larger with a pruning compound or grafting wax to prevent borers from entering wounds. Throughout the season, keep shears handy for small jobs, such as broken branches and shaping. Shears also are good for clipping the sturdy stems of flowers for indoor bouquets.

Climbing 'Blaze' roses frame the view with bright red flowers on this 8-foot-tall, lattice arbor.

Climbing roses are pruned later than bush roses because they bloom on the previous year's growth. Limit spring pruning to cutting out dead canes and trimming branches to a desirable shape. For optimum flowering, train canes horizontally on a trellis by securing canes with plant ties.

After the climber has bloomed, remove two or three of the oldest canes to make room for fresh new growth. Thin out dense growth and shorten the canes on plants that have grown too large. A rose grows where it is cut, so cut canes back farther than you want their final size to be.

Preparing the Soil

Good earth is the key to cultivating beautiful, trouble-free roses. Although bushy by nature, roses are far more finicky about their growing conditions than other traditional landscaping shrubs. Only some of the true shrub roses are rugged enough to flourish with minimal soil preparation.

Soil Tests

To ensure a healthy start for roses, it's important to have your soil tested first. You can purchase a simple kit at a local garden center, or contact your county agricultural extension service for a more in-depth laboratory analysis. Test results will show the levels of nutrients—particularly phosphorus and potassium—present in your soil. If a deficiency is found, add bone meal or superphosphate to the soil.

A soil test will also measure pH, indicated by a number between 0 and 14 on an acidic-basic scale. (The number 7 is neutral, with 0 being the most acidic and 14 most basic.) Roses prefer a pH of 6.0 to 6.5. To raise the pH, add agricultural lime or dolomitic limestone to the soil; to decrease it, add sulfur.

Roses will flourish in any fertile soil that drains well. Amend poor, heavy soils by mixing in organic material.

Good Timing

The best time to prepare a garden for roses is a season or two before you plan to plant them. In the North, for example, you should dig the bed in early autumn, before the ground freezes. That allows soil amendments to blend in over the winter and do their work before spring planting.

Soil should be light and rich to guarantee good growth. With a spade or rotary tiller, turn the earth to a depth of 18 to 24 inches. If the soil is heavy with clay, loosen it by mixing in organic material, such as well-rotted cow manure, compost, or sphagnum peat moss. You should work in enough organic matter to make it about 25 percent of your finished soil. The mineral gypsum also will help turn clay soil into a crumbly loam. Incorporate superphosphate into the soil at planting time to ensure good root growth, but use no other fertilizer when planting.

For container roses, you'll get best results if you use a soil-less potting medium. Commericial potting medium will provide all the nutriments your roses need and will be light enough to make your containers portable.

Drainage

Good drainage is the final test your soil must pass before you begin planting. Even in the most fertile earth, a rosebush will fail to flourish if its feet stay wet. To determine if your garden drains satisfactorily, dig a hole large enough to hold a gallon-size bucket. Fill the hole with water and wait one hour. If the soil has absorbed the water within that time period, then drainage is good. If water still remains, improve drainage by adding coarse sand or vermiculite, setting drainage tiles, or terracing. Growing roses in raised beds, in which soil is loose to several inches below the roots of the bushes, is one of the best ways to ensure adequate drainage.

A well-worn portal offers a rustic backdrop for climbing roses and trumpet vine. Beds brim with impatiens, Mexican evening primrose, coreopsis, and statice.

Feeding Roses

Roses, like people, need a balanced diet to lead a healthy life. Understanding the basics of plant nutrition will help ensure a successful rose feeding program.

To begin, good plant growth requires 16 nutrients, plus minor elements. Of these food groups, nitrogen, phosphorus, and potassium are the most essential, and need to be added regularly to the soil, either through organic or inorganic fertilizers. Nitrogen (N) stimulates the growth of canes, stems, and leaves; phosphorus (P) promotes strong roots and flower production; and potassium (K) contributes to plant vigor for increased resistance to disease and cold temperatures.

A combination of organic and inorganic fertilizers is best for roses, beginning with organic soil amendments and mulch, followed by regular applications of a commercial fertilizer. True organic

Push mulch aside and sprinkle fertilizer evenly around the bush, avoiding contact with the crown. Scratch the fertilizer lightly into the soil, then water. Reapply the mulch.

Century-old farms offer blooming reminders of the rose's roots in American history. A new arbor, opposite, gives this old climber—original to the homestead—a respectful lift.

fertilizers come from animal and plant wastes, such as manures, compost, bone meal, and cottonseed meal. These bulky materials improve soil structure and slowly release nutrients into the soil as they break down.

Inorganic fertilizers are chemicals, such as potassium, ammonium nitrates, and ammonium phosphates. Available in granular or liquid forms, they're fast acting, and must be applied frequently to be effective. In a typical fertilizer formulated especially for roses, you'll see on the label a series of numbers, such as 5-10-5, which stand for the percentages of N, P, and K, in that order.

Feeding Schedule

If your soil is properly prepared, roses require no additional fertilizing at planting time. Wait until the first cycle of blooms fade before you feed the bushes. Fertilize new roses again approximately two months before the first expected fall frost. (Later feeding will only stimulate soft new growth, which is vulnerable to frost damage.) The exception to this rule is in warm climates, where a late-summer feeding ensures a flush of autumn flowers.

Established rosebushes should be fertilized at least three times a year: after pruning in early spring, just before the first bloom, and two months before the first fall frost. Many rose gardeners supplement their regular fertilizing program with a monthly foliar feeding, which involves spraying a liquid fertilizer directly on the leaves to give plants an instant boost. Soluble fertilizers also can be mixed in with a fungicide or insecticide, letting the spray do double duty in half the time.

If you use liquid fertilizers only, apply them every two weeks because they leach from the soil quickly. Apply them to the foliage only if the temperature is below 90 degrees.

Spread the fertilizer evenly over premoistened soil according to label directions. Lightly work it into the top of the soil or mulch, and water well.

Watering Roses

Roses will reward you with vigorous growth and big, showy blooms if you give them the moisture they need. The watering device you use depends on your personal preference, budget, and garden size.

If you're growing just a few roses, watering each plant by hand is a simple task, either with a sprinkling can or a spray nozzle on a garden hose. For a large rose garden, an overhead sprinkler offers ease and automation. Its cleansing shower washes residues and dust from foliage, and discourages spider mites. If you use a sprinkler, run it only in the morning. Rose foliage that is still wet at night is more vulnerable to disease.

A flexible soaker hose, which is left in the garden all season, uses water most efficiently. Tiny pores along the entire length of the hose sweat droplets of water around the base of plants, so little is lost to evaporation. This system keeps foliage dry, reducing the threat of disease.

Regular Watering

Whatever method you choose, water your roses regularly. Roses require one inch of rainfall (or the equivalent in supplemental watering) every week during the growing season. A rain guage will tell you whether or not Mother Nature is providing an adequate amount. During dry spells, water deeply to keep the entire root area of the rose moist.

Your soil type will determine how often you have to turn on the garden hose. In general, sandy soils need to be watered more frequently; clay soils, less. Properly prepared soil is best because, while it allows for drainage, it also retains moisture. To test ground moisture, stick your finger in the soil as far as it will go. If the soil feels dry at fingertip depth, it's time to water.

Mulching

Keep in mind that exposed soil loses moisture quickly to evaporation, especially on hot, windy days. To help the soil retain moisture, mulch rosebushes with a 3- to 4-inch layer of organic material, such as shredded bark, pine needles, cocoa bean hulls, or straw. Don't use peat moss because once dried it's hard to rewet. Mulch also discourages weeds (which compete for water) and enriches the soil as it breaks down. Mulched roses stay cleaner, too, because the ground-level barrier prevents any soil from splattering the foliage and flowers during watering or rainstorms.

For best results, apply mulch in the spring after the ground has warmed. First, lightly cultivate the earth around plants (being careful not to disturb tender feeder roots near the surface) and thoroughly soak the soil. Then, spread the mulch around plants, keeping it from direct contact with the canes.

Perhaps the only disadvantage of mulch is that it depletes the soil of nitrogen as it decomposes. If rose foliage begins to pale, feed plants a nitrogen-rich fertilizer.

Many old garden roses and shrub roses are tougher than modern hybrids. The harsh climate in the high desert garden opposite agrees with such varieties as 'The Fairy,' 'Iceberg,' 'Queen Elizabeth,' 'Betty Prior,' and 'Europeana.'

Always water thoroughly right after planting. Later, use a flexible soaker hose for long-term watering. Tiny pores slowly release droplets of water at ground level around plants. Cover the rose bed with mulch, such as shredded bark.

Keeping Roses Healthy

Potted tree roses stage a summer-long, movable performance. In the fall, pots should be placed in a frost-free location.

Caring for your rose plants throughout the growing season will reward you with colorful displays from spring to fall. To keep the show going, you'll need to remove spent blooms from most roses. Clipping off faded flowers before the petals fall keeps the garden free of debris. It also stimulates a plant to quickly redirect its energy to producing more flower buds. First-year rosebushes, especially, get a boost from deadheading because it encourages vigorous plant growth.

You can leave shrub roses and old garden roses alone after they finish flowering. Their spent blooms form eye-catching red or orange hips that will lure birds to your yard. Climbing roses, too, produce attractive hips. However, you'll be assured a repeat flower performance if you prune climbers as soon as the first flush of blooms has finished. For best results, cut the lateral branches, leaving two five-leaflet leaves on each branch. Within about six weeks, a new stem will grow from each leaf axil and bloom.

Eliminate Suckers

Each time you work in your garden, keep an eye out for fast-growing shoots, called suckers, which emerge from the root stock beneath the bud union of hybrid roses. Suckers are easily identified by their small, often pale, finely serrated leaves. If allowed to grow, suckers quickly can dominate the upper, grafted portion of the plant and sap its energy. When they appear, cut off the shoots as close to the root stock as possible. (You may need to dig down under the soil.) On tree roses, watch for suckers growing from both the main trunk and the root stock; remove them immediately. Miniature roses, old garden roses, and shrub roses grow from their own roots, so suckers are not a threat; in fact, their growth revitalizes the plants.

The power to determine flower size is at your fingertips when you practice a popular technique called disbudding. To foster one showy flower on each stem on hybrid teas or grandifloras, pinch off all the tiny side buds as soon as they form. (If you wait too long to remove them, you'll leave ugly black scars on the plant.) With no competition from the side buds, the central bud receives all the nourishment, allowing it to grow much larger. On floribundas, you can encourage a full floral spray by removing the large central bud as soon as it forms. Here again, don't wait too long, or a hole will be left in the center.

Pest and Disease Basics

Rose foliage needs regular spraying or dusting to prevent a variety of diseases, such as blackspot and mildew. Probably the easiest way to keep your plants healthy is to use a hand duster to apply rose dust every few weeks throughout the growing season.

It's best to treat insect pests such as aphids as they appear. That way you avoid using excessive amounts of pesticides in your garden. In fact, most insects that feed on roses can be controlled easily by spraying the plants with insecticidal soap. The soap will kill the bugs without harming the environment. Japanese beetles can be eliminated safely by applying milky spore diseases to the soil around your rose garden. This biological control infects the beetle larvae living in the soil.

Probably the easiest way to keep your roses healthy is to pull any weeds that grow between the plants. Weeds compete with roses for water and food, and are breeding grounds for insects and diseases. A thick mulch of shredded hardwood bark, pine needles, or leaves will help keep weeds at bay and maintain constant soil moisture. Mulched roses also stay cleaner because the protective covering prevents soil from splattering the foliage during rainstorms.

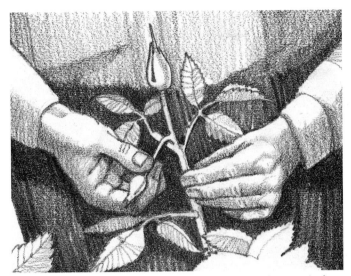

For large, one-bloom-per-stem flowers on hybrid teas, pinch off all side flower buds as soon as they appear. Don't wait too long; you'll leave black scars. For showier floribunda sprays, remove the central buds as they form.

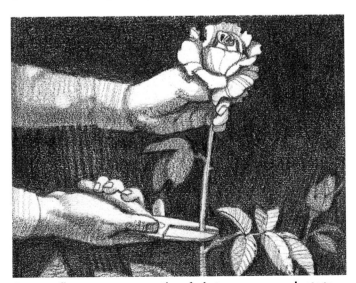

Remove flowers as soon as they fade to encourage plants to produce more blooms. Make the cuts at 45-degree angles above strong, five-leaflet leaves. Preserve at least two sets of leaves on each cane to maintain plant vigor.

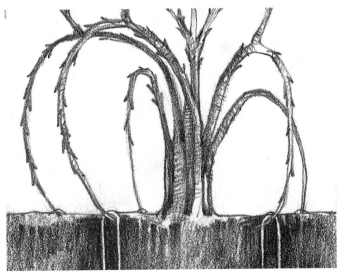

Make a sprawling shrub rose look full by arching the canes to the ground, and securing them to the soil with hoops of heavy wire. Eventually, the canes will root where they touch the ground; new growth will start from the tops of the arches.

Winter Protection

The amount of winter care you give your roses depends on your climate, their placement in the yard, and the types of roses you grow. Drying winds and fluctuating weather—not prolonged periods of subzero temperatures—are the biggest culprits of dieback. In fact, roses often survive winters with less damage in cold, snowy areas than they do in milder regions where snowfall and temperatures are erratic.

A constant cover of snow is nature's own best protection. Winter survival can vary even within a neighborhood. Plants grown in a shielded location, for example, usually will fare better than those without shelter from cold winds.

Tender roses—China, tea, and most pastel hybrid teas, floribundas, and grandifloras—require protection if winter temperatures drop below freezing. The best time to cover roses for winter is right after the ground has frozen.

Mounding Soil

One time-honored way to protect plants is to mound soil over the canes to a height of 20 inches. Soil should be taken from another part of the garden to avoid injuring the shallow feeder roots of your roses.

In early spring, remove the mound of soil as soon as the buds swell, before tender new growth begins. First, wash away soil from the crown with a gentle stream from the garden hose. (The bud union should end up being visible just above ground level.) Then, remove the rest of the soil mound with a small spade or trowel.

The downside to the mounding method is that soil settles and erodes during the winter, gradually exposing canes to cold, drying winds. For this reason, many rose gardeners prefer surrounding each plant with a wire mesh cylinder, and filling the inside of the cylinder with a loose, organic material, such as shredded bark or leaves. (Oak leaves are best; avoid maple leaves, which mat down and form an inpenetrable barrier for moisture.) In the spring, remove the cage and spread the material over the bed for mulch.

Plastic Foam Cones

Rose cones are the most popular prefabricated products available for winter protection. Made of plastic foam, these insulative covers are placed over individual plants. During the growing season, cones can be stacked and stored for use again the following winter.

The drawback to rose cones is that they act like miniature greenhouses during winter warm spells, stimulating growth that will be nipped off when cold weather returns. To avoid this problem, remove the covers on mild days. Because canes must be heavily pruned to fit under a rose cone, this method of protection is recommended only for the most tender hybrids in the coldest climates.

Winter Challenge

Tree roses pose a tall challenge because the tender bud union is located high above the ground, where it is very susceptible to winter damage. You can wrap a tree or you can bury it in the ground by digging a trench on one side of the plant. On the opposite side of the plant, use a spade to loosen the roots. Bend the plant down to the trench, securing the trunk to the ground with crossed stakes. Cover the entire plant with mounded soil. Many gardeners grow tree roses in pots so the pots can be moved to a frost-free area.

Hardy roses require little, if any, winter protection. Shrub roses and old garden roses can withstand temperatures as low as minus 10 degrees. Polyanthas are very hardy, withstanding the rigors of almost any winter. Miniature roses are tough, too, but they benefit from a blanket of leaves raked around them.

Most climbers tolerate temperatures below 20 degrees, but if the mercury dips below zero in your area, you'll need to take the canes off their supports and bury them in the ground (as illustrated, opposite). Or wrap the canes in burlap where they are attached to the trellis. (This method can be cumbersome and difficult to manage.) In early spring, remove the protection and tie the climbers back up to the supports.

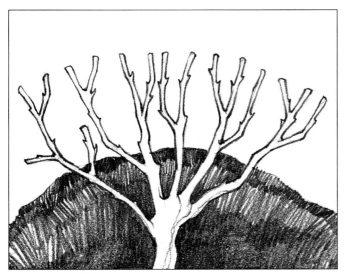

Mounding soil over the canes to a height of 20 inches is the traditional way to protect hybrid roses. Bring the soil from another part of the garden to avoid damaging tender roots. Remove the soil in spring, before new growth starts.

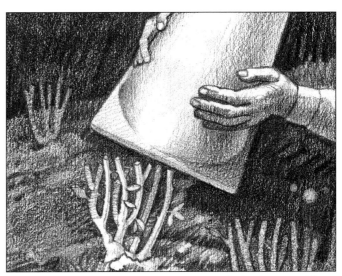

In the coldest parts of the country, protect hybrid roses with plastic foam cones. Wait until the ground freezes before covering the plants. Remove the cones on warm winter days to keep excess heat from stimulating plant growth too early.

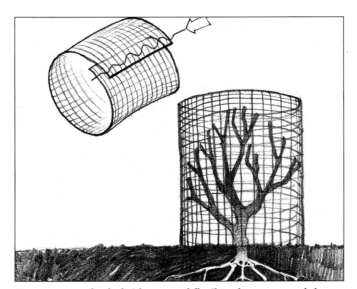

To protect tender hybrid teas and floribundas, surround them with a wire cone. Fill the area inside the wire cone with leaves. The cone will prevent the leaves from blowing away and will keep rabbits from gnawing on the canes.

Where temperatures drop below zero, take climber canes off their supports and secure them to the ground with crossed stakes. Cover the canes with mounded soil. Or, leave the canes in place and wrap them in burlap and leaves.

Pests and Diseases

It's only natural for rose gardeners to strive for perfect plants and flawless flowers. Unfortunately, pests and diseases often try to interfere and ruin the show.

The best defense against unwanted invasions is fostering good health, which begins with well-prepared soil, proper fertilizing, adequate watering, and a garden that's free of weeds and debris. You also can select disease-resistant rose varieties. Keep in mind, though, that these hybrids fend off diseases under normal conditions, but they're not completely immune. All roses benefit from some preventive care offered by a regular application of chemical controls. Fortunately, modern equipment and ready-to-use products make pest and disease prevention and control an easy task.

The charts on the following pages will help you identify the most common rose pests and diseases. Insecticides are used to control insect pests. They're generally applied as needed, after the first signs of attack.

Fungicides, in contrast, are formulated to protect rose plants from diseases. They are a preventive treatment, not a cure, so their application must start before a disease strikes. Most rose gardeners adopt a regular fungicide program, spraying or dusting plants every 10 days throughout the growing season.

Choosing Chemicals

For best results, choose the correct products for your particular rose problems. Read labels to determine which diseases and insect pests each product is formulated to treat. Or, to save time, seek the advice of a trained professional at your local garden center.

For the sake of convenience, many rose gardeners purchase an all-purpose combination of chemicals specially formulated for roses. These premixed products contain a pesticide, fungicide, and miticide, freeing your garden shed of a large, and sometimes confusing, assortment of bottles and brews. Never combine different chemicals yourself unless it has been specifically recommended by the manufacturer.

Chemical controls are available in liquid or dust forms. The form you choose depends on your situation and the type of equipment you prefer using. For a few roses, you may find that dust is easier because it requires no mixing. Simply pour the powder in a duster and use it whenever necessary, without having to clean the duster between applications.

A liquid spray is more effective than dusting because it covers plants more uniformly. Ready-to-use trigger sprayers are good for small gardens. For a dozen or more roses, choose between hose-end diluting sprayers or refillable pump sprayers.

Reading Labels

Before you apply any chemicals, read the label carefully. Mix and apply only as directed; avoid the temptation to make a stronger concoction or spray more frequently than advised. Most importantly, comply with all precautions listed with any chemical product. Choose an overcast and calm morning to apply both dusts and sprays.

Dusting may be done before the dew dries because the moisture will help the dust stick to the leaves. Wait until after the dew has dried before you do any spraying. Apply an even spray to both the tops and undersides of foliage until liquid starts to drip off the leaves.

Cleaning Up

After you have finished spraying, rinse out the sprayer thoroughly with clear water to prevent corrosion. Do not save the leftover solution for future use; instead, mix up a fresh batch each time you spray. Avoid using your sprayer for other chemical applications, such as weed killers. The residues they leave in the sprayer, however small, might burn your rose plants the next time you spray them. Store all chemicals in a safe place, beyond the reach of children and pets

Planted along a low fence, 'Cecil Brunner' and climbing white 'Iceberg' roses create a streetside bouquet.

Rose Diseases

DISEASE	DESCRIPTION AND TROUBLE SIGNS	CONTROLS
Black spot	A fungus disease, it causes rounded black spots to appear on the foliage. Eventually, a yellow halo forms around the black spot, after which the entire leaf turns yellow and falls off. The disease is spread by splashing water.	When you prune, throw away all clippings, which may harbor black spot spores. Avoid watering plant from above. Use a commercial fungicide.
Botrytis	The fungus often keeps buds from opening, covering them with grayish brown, fuzzy growth. If buds do open, flowers are flecked with yellow or brown, and the petals become soft and brown. The problem is most severe under cool, humid conditions.	Cut out and destroy all infected plant parts. Preventive sprays often are ineffective. The fungus usually disappears when weather improves.
Canker	A fungus disease, it attacks canes. Cankers are noticeable in early spring at pruning time. The lower part of the cane is green and healthy, but above the healthy part is a black, brown, or purple discoloration. Canker usually enters through a wound.	In spring, prune off and discard canes to below signs of canker. Prevent wounds by using sharp shears. Dip shears in alcohol after each use to stop spread of disease. There is no chemical control.
Crown gall	The bacterium stunts growth and reduces flowering. Rough, round growths are found around the roots at or below the soil surface.	Prune small galls, disinfecting pruning shears between cuts. In severe cases, discard the plant.

DISEASE	DESCRIPTION AND TROUBLE SIGNS	CONTROLS
Mildew, downy	Downy mildew causes foliage to develop purplish red to dark brown irregular spots. Leaves turn yellow and eventually fall off. This fungus also causes gray, fuzzy growth on the undersides of the leaves.	Spray with a fungicide every seven to 10 days to prevent downy mildew. Remove and discard any infected leaves.
Mosaic	Fungus forms a white powder on rosebuds and leaves. It is most prevalent when nights are cool and days are warm, or where air circulation is poor. Mildew often causes serious disfiguration of the foliage.	Mosaic symptoms often disappear by themselves. In severe cases, remove the plant. There are no chemical controls.
Rust	A virus, it causes foliage to become mottled in yellow or develop a yellow netting or streaking. Growth becomes less vigorous, and the plants are more prone to winterkill.	Inspect all new bushes and avoid planting any that show signs of rust. Control with a commercial fungicide. Remove infected leaves.
Spot anthracnose	A fungus starts with development of red, brown, or purple spots on the upper leaves. The centers of these spots eventually turn white, dry, and fall out. Affected leaves turn yellow and fall off.	Spray with a fungicide every seven days as long as symptoms persist. Avoid watering the plant from above.

Rose Pests

INSECT	DESCRIPTION AND TROUBLE SIGNS	CONTROLS
Aphids	Also called plant lice, aphids are tiny but visible green or brown insects that form colonies along flower buds and new shoot growth, starting in mid- to late spring. They harm roses by sucking their vital juices. A sticky substance called honeydew may appear on the leaves.	Knock aphids off the plant with a strong stream of water from the garden hose. Or spray with soapy water or a commercial insecticide.
Borers	Borers tunnel into canes and under the bark, hollowing out the pith and killing the shoot. Wilting of the top of the plant often indicates the presence of the borer. The cane usually will swell where the borer is hiding.	Prune just below each swelling, then apply a sealing compound. Be careful not to injure canes when working in the garden.
Japanese beetles	Shiny copper and green, ¼-inch insects can devour an entire garden in a short time. They eat holes in the flowers, particularly white and pastel ones. If hungry enough, they also eat the leaves.	Remove beetles by hand if invasion is light. Traps are effective, but often attract more beetles to the garden. Control grubs in the soil for best results.
Leaf-cutting bees	Leaf-cutting bees cut neat circles into the edges of the leaves. The bees do not eat these leaf pieces, but rather use them to build their nests.	Prune severely damaged canes. Since leaf-cutting bees do not eat the foliage, chemicals are ineffective.
Leaf rollers	Green or yellow caterpillars that grow to 1 inch long roll themselves up in the rose leaves and eat through them from the inside out. Another sign of these pests is tiny holes in the base of the flower buds.	Use chemical insecticides or organic controls for maximum effectiveness.

INSECT	DESCRIPTION AND TROUBLE SIGNS	CONTROLS
Midges	A tiny insect maggot, it bores into a rose plant, causing the buds and the new shoots to suddenly blacken and die.	Prune the damage immediately and discard it. Spray a commercial insecticide on the tops of the plants and apply a systemic insecticide to the ground around the plants.
Nematodes	The microscopic worms cause disease symptoms in roses. Small knotty growths develop on the roots. Plants lose their vigor. Leaves turn yellow, wilt, and fall. Flowers become smaller.	Discard infested plants, and do not plant roses in the same spot for a few years. Professional treatment of soil may be needed.
Rose scales	The gray, brown, or white hard-shelled insects encrust the stems and suck sap from the branches. Growth is stunted and flowers don't form. Plants eventually wilt and die.	Prune and discard infested canes. Spray with dormant oil in early spring and with commercial systemic insecticide as insects appear in summer.
Rose slugs	Small, soft, yellow-green caterpillarlike pests, they eat the foliage, leaving skeletons. Rose slugs can bore into the pith of pruned canes.	Spray rose slugs with a commercial insecticide as soon as signs of damage appear.
Spider mites	The spider mite is too small to see, but its effects are obvious. Technically, it's not an insect, but it does the damage of one. Foliage turns dry and bronze or dull red. In advanced stages, webs can be seen. Spider mites weaken roses by sucking juices from foliage.	Because spider mites do not like water, keep plants well watered, and hose down the undersides of foliage. For heavy infestations, apply a miticide three times at three-day intervals.

Propagating Roses

New and improved rose varieties are not simply accidental finds made by rose growers. They are products of years of careful observation, research, skill, and hard work by hybridizers. Luck may play a small part in the development of an outstanding new rose, but few rose growers depend on it. Researchers must have an intimate knowledge of which roses have good parents, which good and bad traits are passed on most frequently, and which combinations are most likely to produce the desired offspring.

Once you've mastered the art of growing roses, you may want to branch out and learn about the science of cultivating new hybrids. The cultivars you create in your own rose garden may never win a prize, but they'll deepen your understanding of the complex life cycle of roses and help you appreciate what an enormous accomplishment it is when professional rose breeders introduce an improved variety to the public.

Producing Seeds

The first step in creating a new hybrid is to produce seeds by artificial pollination. To begin, choose two different plants to be your pollen and seed parents. Pair up plants that will offer a desirable combination of traits, such as disease resistance, vigorous growth, color breakthrough, abundant blooming, fragrance, perfect flower form, dark-green foliage, and hardiness. Select the pollen parent first; the flower should be just beginning to open. With small scissors or tweezers, snip off the yellow pollen-bearing stamens from the flower, carefully placing them on a piece of wax paper. Store in a box or glass jar in the refrigerator until the stamens shed the dustlike pollen.

When the pollen is ready, select a second flower—the seed parent—and remove its sepals, petals, and stamens. When the remaining stigma is receptive, or sticky, place pollen on the pistils with a small, sterile paintbrush or cotton swab to induce the setting of seed. Cover the pollinated flower with a small paper bag, secured with a twist-tie, to prevent unwanted pollination by insects. Record the names of the parent plants and the date of pollination. In about two weeks, the receptacle or hip will begin to enlarge, a sure sign that seeds are being produced. The seed pod is ripe and ready to harvest when it turns red or orange, approximately three months later. At this time, you can remove the seeds and plant them immediately in a lightweight potting medium. Or, if you don't have a greenhouse for winter seed starting, you can store the seeds in the refrigerator and wait until spring to plant. In any case, when the new seedlings start to bloom (often within six weeks), thin out the poor performers and keep only the strongest ones.

Grafting Plants

To nurture a promising seedling, you'll need to graft it to a hardy understock plant, such as *Rosa multiflora* or 'Dr. Huey.' Cut a flowering stem (called budwood) from the young seedling after the first flush of blooms fade. From this budwood, remove all the foliage, except for a short leaf stem for a "handle." The growth bud at the leaf axil (where the leaf joins the main stem) of this handle will be grafted to the understock plant.

Slice the bud and handle from the seedling stem, then slide the bud into a T-shape slit that you make in the bark of the understock plant near soil level. Wrap the bud to the understock with a rubberband to hold it in place and prevent it from drying out. If the bud fails to grow, graft a new one to the understock. Once a bud starts to grow on its own, cut back the whole top of the understock plant to within ½ inch of the graft. From then on, the understock will nourish the developing bud growth, and the grafted plant will mature into a new rose.

Only a small percentage of professionally crossbred seedlings are chosen to be budded. The seedlings then are grown and critiqued in trial gardens for two years or more in a wide range of climates. Through a meticulous process of elimination, the most superior new roses make it to the marketable stage. The whole process, from seeding to selling a new hybrid, can take up to 10 years.

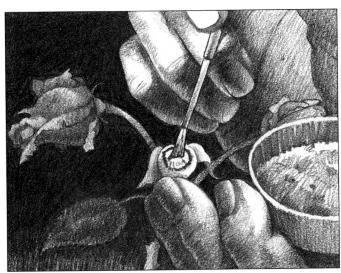

With a small brush, place pollen gathered from the first flower on the pistils of the second flower. Cover the pollinated flower with a small paper bag, secured with a twist-tie, to prevent unwanted pollination by insects.

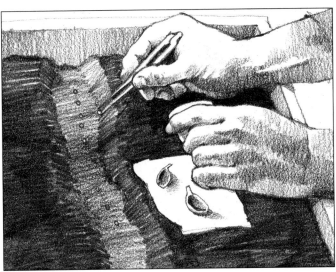

Harvest the rose hip (seed pod) as soon as it turns red or orange. Cut open the pod and remove the seeds, then plant the seeds in a sterile, lightweight potting medium. When the seedlings start to bloom, select the best ones to grow on.

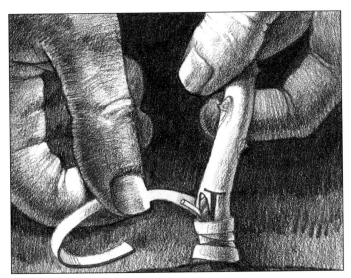

Slice off a portion from a seedling's stem that includes a growth bud (at a leaf axil) and a "handle" of the leaf stem. Fit this bud into a T-shape slit made in the bark of the under-stock plant. Hold the bud in place with a rubber band.

A successfully budded seedling remains plump and green after it has been grafted to the understock plant. As soon as the bud begins to grow on its own, cut back the top of the understock plant to within about ½ inch of the graft.

Cut Roses

Bouquets bring the beauty of your garden indoors. Whether you're displaying a single stem in a crystal bud vase or a dozen in an old crock, the elegance and sweet fragrance of roses are unsurpassed by any other flower.

You can combine roses of different kinds and colors, or stay true to just one type and hue. Colors that harmonize and blend into each other create a more formal look. A variety of bolder, contrasting blooms are more casual, especially when you mix in a handful of other garden flowers, too.

Good companions for roses include iris, lily, delphinium, gladiolus, veronica, snapdragon, salvia, astilbe, aster, daisy, baby's-breath, and zinnia. Be sure to fill out the bouquet with some greenery. Iris, gladiolus, canna, hosta, artemisia, ferns, holly, and pine offer attractive foliage.

Containers

Any container that holds water will do. For a more elegant setting, choose silver, porcelain, crystal, or china. Or be more informal with pewter, pottery, or lined baskets. In shallow containers, you'll need to use florists' foam or a pinholder to keep stems straight and upright.

Arranging flowers in a bouquet is much like combining them in the garden: Choose compatible colors, vary heights, and avoid crowding. For better balance, place darker colored blooms and more fully opened buds toward the bottom, and lighter hues and tighter buds toward the top. If your bouquet will be viewed from all sides, design it accordingly.

You can prolong the life of your bouquet by replacing the water daily, each time adding a floral preservative to the water. Display the arrangement away from direct sunlight and hot or cold drafts to keep blooms from wilting prematurely. If just a few flowers begin to droop, try reviving them by recutting the stems under water.

Overflowing with elegance, a pair of ceramic pitchers are the perfect complement to a breathtaking array of cut roses.

A breezy porch provides an informal setting for a casual arrangement of roses. Nearby, potted lobelia, violas, daisies, and geraniums nod their approval.

One of the joys of growing roses is cutting them for bouquets. Your garden can supply more variety than any florist's shop. When the blooms are nurtured and arranged by your own hands, a gift of roses has greater value.

Long stems are the first quality you should look for in any cutting flower. Hybrid teas are the traditional bouquet roses, forming large, fragrant blooms at the tips of 2- to 5-foot-high stems. Tall cutting

stems are also the hallmark of the regal grandifloras. Although it's tempting to cut stems as long as possible, remember to leave at least two five-leaflet leaves on the stem that remains on the plant to renew growth and ensure future flowering.

Best Bouquets

Varieties with full-petaled, double blossoms are best for bouquets because they last longer in a vase. Those with single blooms open and fade more quickly. Avoid picking the flowers from shrub roses and old garden roses because they'll wilt soon after they're cut. The orange and red hips, however, bring colorful embellishments to autumn arrangements. Don't take any more leaves than necessary if you want your rosebush to keep producing new bloom.

The best time to harvest roses is late afternoon, after the morning dew has dried and the tight buds have begun to open from the day's warmth. If you plan to cut just a few stems, carry them indoors with the flowers head down and place them in water immediately.

For many flowers, you'll need to carry a bucket of lukewarm water (never cold water from the garden hose) to the garden. Cut each stem at an angle and put it in the water up to the neck of the flower. After you have finished gathering flowers, recut the stems under water to aid absorption. Place the pail in a cool, shaded spot for several hours until the water cools to room temperature.

Preparing the Stems

Once your roses are properly conditioned, you can begin preparing the stems for arranging. Snip off torn or chewed leaves, as well as all leaves that would be below the waterline of the bouquet. If left to disintegrate, foliage will foul the water and diminish the flower show.

Wash off spray residues, dust, and mildew from the remaining leaves with soap and water, then rub the leaves with a cloth to restore their natural sheen. To avoid painful pricks, be sure to remove the thorns where you will be holding the stems when you arrange the flowers.

Be selective when you cut roses for a bouquet. Avoid cutting stems with buds so tight that they'll never open, as well as fully open blooms that will soon wilt. The perfect bloom (center) is one that is slightly open with the sepals down.

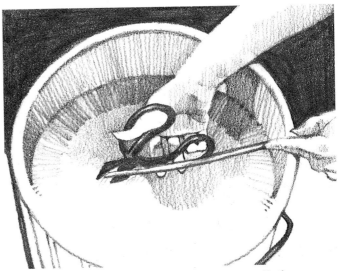

Cut stems at an angle and plunge them into a pail of lukewarm water immediately. (The water should be deep enough to reach just below the flower heads.) Recut the stems under water to help them absorb the moisture.

Clip off all foliage that would otherwise be below the water level in the finished arrangement. Leaves left in the water quickly decay and foul the water, shortening the life of the bouquet. Remove all ripped or damaged leaves, too.

Use florists' tape around each bud to gently hold the blooms shut until you're ready to display the bouquet. To prolong the show, place the arrangement in a cool location, away from direct sunlight and drying drafts.

Consider Your Climate

The key to successful gardening is knowing what plants are best suited to your area and when to plant them. This is true for every type of gardening. Climate maps, such as the one opposite, give a good idea of the extremes in temperature by zones. The zone-number listings tell you the coldest temperature a plant typically can endure.

By choosing plants best adapted to the different zones, and by planting them at the right time, you will have many more successes.

The climate in your area is a mixture of many different weather patterns: sun, snow, rain, wind, and humidity. To be a good gardener, you should know, on an average, how cold the garden gets in winter, how much rainfall it receives each year, and how hot or dry it becomes in a typical summer. You can obtain this general information from your state agricultural school or your county extension agent. In addition, acquaint yourself with the miniclimates in your neighborhood, based on such factors as wind protection gained from a nearby hill, or humidity and cooling offered by a local lake or river. Then carry the research further by studying the microclimates that characterize your own plot of ground.

Key Points to Keep in Mind:

- Plants react to exposure. Southern and western exposures are sunnier and warmer than northern or eastern ones. Light conditions vary greatly even in a small yard. Match your plants' needs to the correct exposure.

- Wind can damage many plants, by either drying the soil or knocking over fragile growth. Protect plants from both summer and winter winds to increase their odds of survival and to save yourself the time and energy of staking plants and watering more frequently.

- Consider elevation, too, when selecting plants. Cold air sweeps down hills and rests in low areas. These frost pockets are fine for some plantings, deadly for others. Plant vegetation that prefers a warmer environment on the tops or sides of hills, never at the bottom.

- Use fences, the sides of buildings, shrubs, and trees to your advantage. Watch the play of shadows, the sweep of winds, and the flow of snowdrifts in winter. These varying situations are ideal for some plants, harmful to others. In short, always look for ways to make the most of everything your yard has to offer.

THE USDA PLANT HARDINESS MAP
OF THE UNITED STATES AND CANADA

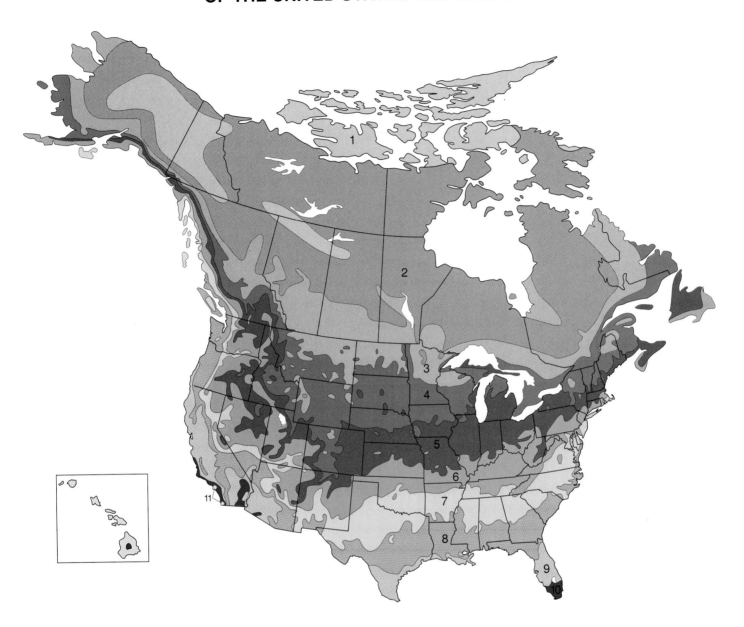

RANGE OF AVERAGE ANNUAL MINIMUM
TEMPERATURES FOR EACH ZONE

	ZONE 1	BELOW -50° F
	ZONE 2	-50° TO -40°
	ZONE 3	-40° TO -30°
	ZONE 4	-30° TO -20°
	ZONE 5	-20° TO -10°
	ZONE 6	-10° TO 0°
	ZONE 7	0° TO 10°
	ZONE 8	10° TO 20°
	ZONE 9	20° TO 30°
	ZONE 10	30° TO 40°
	ZONE 11	ABOVE 40°

Public Rose Gardens

ALABAMA
Birmingham
The Formal Rose Garden
Birmingham Botanical Gardens
Fairhope
Fairhope City Rose Garden
Mobile
Battleship Memorial Park
David A. Hemphill Park of Roses
Mobile Public Rose Garden
Theodore
Bellingrath Gardens Rose Garden

ARIZONA
Glendale
Fields D.D.S. & Associates Rose Garden
Sahuaro Historical Ranch Rose Garden
Phoenix
Encanto Park Rose Garden
Valley Garden Center Rose Garden
Tucson
Gene C. Reid Park

ARKANSAS
Little Rock
State Capitol Rose Garden

CALIFORNIA
Berkeley
Berkeley Municipal Rose Garden
Beverly Hills
Virginia Robinson Gardens
Citrus Heights
Fountain Square Rose Garden
Corona del Mar
Roger's Gardens
Sherman Library and Gardens
DeLano
Bella Rosa Winery Rose Garden
Encinitas
Quail Botanical Gardens
La Canada
Descanso Gardens Rose Garden
Los Angeles
Exposition Park Rose Garden

Malibu
J. Paul Getty Museum
Oakland
Morcom Amphitheater of Roses
Palos Verdes Peninsula
South Coast Botanic Garden
James J. White Rose Garden
Pasadena
Rose Bowl Rose Garden
Tournament of Roses Wrigley Garden
Riverside
Fairmount Park Rose Garden
Sacramento
Capitol Park Rose Garden
McKinley Park Rose Garden
San Diego
Inez Curant Parker Memorial Rose Garden
San Francisco
Golden Gate Park Rose Garden
San Jose
San Jose Municipal Rose Garden
San Marino
Huntington Botanical Gardens
San Simeon
Hearst San Simeon State Historical Monument
Santa Barbara
A.C. Postel Memorial Rose Garden
Wasco
Wasco Community Garden
Westminster
Westminster Civic Center Rose Garden
Whittier
Pageant of Roses Garden
Rose Hills Memorial Park
Woodside
Filoli Center

COLORADO
Durango
Four Corners Rose Garden
Littleton
War Memorial Rose Garden

Longmont
Longmont Memorial Rose Garden

CONNECTICUT
Norwich
Norwich Memorial Rose Garden
West Hartford
Elizabeth Park Rose Garden

DELAWARE
Wilmington
Hagley Museum and Library

DISTRICT OF COLUMBIA
Dumbarton Oaks
The George Washington University
The United States Botanic Garden

FLORIDA
Cypress Gardens
Florida Cypress Gardens
Davenport
Giles Rose Nursery
Lake Buena Vista
Walt Disney World Resort
Largo
Sturgeon Memorial Rose Garden
Okeechokee
Giles Ramblin' Roses Nursery

GEORGIA
Athens
Elizabeth Bradley Turner Memorial Rose Garden
The State Botanical Garden of Georgia
Atlanta
Atlanta Botanical Garden
Thomasville
Thomasville Nurseries, Inc. Rose Test Garden

HAWAII
Honolulu
Queen Kapiolani Park
Kula, Maui
Maui Agricultural Research Center
University of Hawaii

IDAHO
Boise
Julia Davis Memorial Rose Garden

ILLINOIS
Alton
The Gordon F. Moore Community Park
The Nan Elliot Memorial Rose Garden
Chicago
Marquette Park Rose Garden
Evanston
Merrick Park Rose Garden
Glencoe
The Bruce Krasberg Rose Garden
Chicago Botanic Garden
Highland Park
Park District of Highland Park
Libertyville
Lynn J. Arthur Rose Garden
Lisle
The Morton Arboretum
Peoria
George L. Luthy Memorial Botanical Garden
Rockford
Sinnissippi Greenhouse and Gardens
Springfield
Washington Park Rose Garden
Wheaton
Cantigny Gardens

INDIANA
Fort Wayne
Lakeside Rose Garden
Richmond
Richmond Rose Garden

IOWA
Ames
Iowa State University Horticultural Garden
Bettendorf
Charles Liebestein Memorial Rose Garden
Cedar Rapids
Noelridge Park Rose Garden
Clinton
Bickelhaupt Arboretum

Davenport
VanderVeer Park Municipal Rose Garden
Des Moines
Greenwood Park Rose Garden
Dubuque
Dubuque Arboretum and Botanical Gardens
Muscatine
Weed Park Memorial Rose Garden
State Center
State Center Public Rose Garden

KANSAS
Gage Park
Lake Shawnee Gardens
Topeka
E.F.A. Reinisch Rose Garden

KENTUCKY
Louisville
Kentucky Memorial Rose Garden

LOUISIANA
Baton Rouge
Louisiana State University Agriculture Center
   All-America Rose Society Rose Garden
Many
Hodges Gardens
Shreveport
American Rose Center

MAINE
Portland
City of Portland Rose Circle

MARYLAND
Annapolis
William Paca Garden
Baltimore
Maryland Rose Society Heritage Rose Garden
The Cylburn Arboretum
Monkton
Ladew Topiary Gardens
Wheaton
Brookside Botanical Gardens Rose Garden

MASSACHUSETTS
Boston
James P. Kelleher Rose Garden
Jamaica Plain
Arnold Arboretum of Harvard University
Stockbridge
Berkshire Garden Center
Westfield
The Stanley Park of Westfield, Inc.

MICHIGAN
Ann Arbor
Matthaei Botanical Gardens
University of Michigan
Detroit
Anna Scripps Whitcomb Conservatory
East Lansing
Michigan State University Horticultural
   Demonsration Gardens
Lansing
Frances Park Memorial Rose Garden
Niles
Fernwood Botanic Gardens
Wayne
Wayne County Cooperative Extension Garden

MINNESOTA
Channhassen
Minnesota Landscape Arboretum
Minneapolis
Lyndale Park Municipal Rose Garden
St. Paul
Como Park Conservatory

MISSISSIPPI
Hattiesburg
Hattiesburg Area Rose Society Garden
   University of Southern Mississippi
Jackson
The Jim Buck Ross Rose Garden
Mississippi Agriculture and Forestry Museum

MISSOURI
Cape Girardeau
Cape Girardeau Rose Display Garden

Kansas City
Laura Conyers Smith Municipal Rose Garden
Jacob L. Loose Memorial Park
St. Louis
Gladney & Lehmann Rose Gardens
Missouri Botanical Garden

MONTANA
Missoula
Missoula Memorial Rose Garden

NEBRASKA
Boys Town
Boys Town AARS Constitution Rose Garden
Lincoln
Lincoln Municipal Rose Garden
Omaha
Hanscom Park Greenhouse
Memorial Park Rose Garden

NEVADA
Reno
Reno Municipal Rose Garden

NEW HAMPSHIRE
North Hampton
Fuller Gardens Rose Gardens

NEW JERSEY
Bloomfield
Brookdale Park Rose Garden
East Millstone
Rudolf V. van der Goot Rose Garden
Colonial Park
Lincroft
Lambertus C. Bobbink Memorial Garden
Morristown
Freylinghuysen Arboretum
Summit
The Reeves-Reed Arboretum
Tenafly
Jack D. Lissemore Rose Garden
Davis Johnson Park & Gardens
NEW MEXICO
Albuquerque
Prospect Park Rose Garden

NEW YORK
Bronx
The Peggy Rockefeller Rose Garden
The New York Botanical Garden
Brooklyn
Cranford Rose Garden
Brooklyn Botanical Garden
Buffalo
Joan Fuzak Memorial Rose Garden
Delaware Park
Canadaigua
Sonnenberg Gardens Rose Garden

Flushing
Queens Botanical Garden
Fort Tryon Park
The Cloisters
The Metropolitan Museum of Art
New York
United Nations Rose Garden
Old Westbury
Old Westbury Gardens
Rochester
Maplewood Rose Garden
Schenectady
Central Park Rose Garden
Syracuse
Dr. E. M. Mills Memorial Rose Garden
Thorden Park

NORTH CAROLINA
Asheville
Biltmore Estate
Clemmons
Tanglewood Park Rose Garden
Fayetteville
Fayetteville Rose Garden
Raleigh
Raleigh Municipal Rose Garden
Winston-Salem
Reynolda Rose Gardens of Wake Forest
  University
NORTH DAKOTA
Dunseith
International Peace Garden, Inc.

OHIO
Akron
Stan Hywet Hall and Gardens
Bay Village
Cahoon Memorial Rose Garden
Cleveland
Mary Anne Sears Sweetland Rose Garden
Columbus
Columbus Park of Roses
Mansfield
Charles E. Nail Memorial Rose Garden
Westerville
Inniswood Metro Gardens
Wooster
Secrest Arboretum, Ohio State University
Youngstown
Fellows Riverside Gardens

OKLAHOMA
Muskogee
J.E. Conrad Municipal Rose Garden
Oklahoma City
Charles E. Sparks Rose Garden
Tulsa
Tulsa Municipal Rose Garden

OREGON
Coos Bay
Shore Acres Botanical Garden/State Park
Corvallis
Corvallis Rose Garden, Avery Park
Eugene
Owen Memorial Rose Garden
Portland
International Rose Test Garden

PENNSYLVANIA
Allentown
Malcolm W. Gross Memorial Rose Garden
Hershey
Hershey Gardens
Kennett Square
Longwood Gardens, Inc.
McKeesport
Garden Club of McKeesport

Philadelphia
Marion Rivanus Rose Garden
Morris Arboretum
West Grove
Robert Pyle Memorial Rose Gardens

RHODE ISLAND
Bristol
Blithewolde Gardens and Arboretum
Newport
Rosecliff

SOUTH CAROLINA
Orangeburg
Edisto Memorial Gardens

SOUTH DAKOTA
Rapid City
Rapid City Memorial Rose Garden
Halby Park

TENNESSEE
Chattanooga
Warner Park Rose Garden
Memphis
Memphis Municipal Rose Garden
Nashville
Cheekwood Botanical Gardens

TEXAS
Austin
Mabell Davis Rose Garden
Zilker Botanical Gardens
Dallas
Samuell-Grand Municipal Rose Garden
El Paso
El Paso Municipal Rose Garden
Fort Worth
Fort Worth Botanic Gardens
Houston
Houston Municipal Rose Garden

Tyler
Tyler Municipal Rose Garden
Victoria
Victoria Rose Garden

UTAH
Farmington
Utah Botanical Garden
Fillmore
Territorial Statehouse State Park Rose Garden
Nephi
Nephi Federated Women's Club Memorial
 Rose Garden
Salt Lake City
Salt Lake Municipal Rose Garden

VIRGINIA
Alexandria
River Farm Garden, American Horticultural
 Society
Woodlawn Plantation
Arlington
Bon Air Park Memorial Rose Garden
Lynchburg
Confederate Section, Old City Cemetery
Norfolk
Norfolk Botanical Garden Bicentennial
 Rose Garden

WASHINGTON
Bellingham
Cornwall Park Rose Garden

RESOURCES
Roses
Edmunds' Roses
6235 S.W. Kahle Rd.
Wilsonville, OR 97070
503/682-1476
Gardener's Supply Company
128 Intervale Rd.
Burlington, VT 05401-2850
802/863-1700
Gurney's Seed & Nursery Co.
110 Capitol St.
Yankton, SD 57079
1/605-665-1930
Inter-State Nurseries
1800 Hamilton Rd.
Bloomington, IL 61704
309/663-9551

Jackson & Perkins
1 Rose Lane
Medford, OR 97501-0702
1/800-USA-ROSE
Nor'East Miniature Roses, Inc.
P.O. Box 307
Rowley, MA 01969
1/800-426-6485
Roses of Thomasville
P.O. Box 7
Thomasville, GA 31799
912/226-5568
Roses of Yesterday and Today
Watsonville, CA 95076-0398
408/724-2755
Smith & Hawken
25 Corte Madera
Mill Valley, CA 94941
415/383-2000
Springhill Nurseries
110 W. Elm St.
Tipp City, OH 45371
309/691-4616
Stark Brothers Nursery
Louisiana, MO 63353
Wayside Gardens
1 Garden Lane
Hodges, SC 29695-0001
1/800-845-1124
White Flower Farm
Litchfield, CT 06759-0050
1/800-944-9624

Rose Organizations
All-America Rose Selections, Inc.
221 N. LaSalle St., Suite 3900
Chicago, IL 60601
312/372-7090
American Rose Society
P.O. Box 3900
Shreveport, LA 71130-0030
318/938-5402

Index